Dear Reader:

The book you ar[e]... St. Martin's Tru[e]... *Times* calls "the [...]" you a fascinating [...] that has captured the national attention. St. Martin's is the publisher of perennial bestselling true crime author Jack Olsen (SON and DOC) whose SALT OF THE EARTH is the true story of how one woman fought and triumphed over life-shattering violence; Joseph Wambaugh called it "powerful and absorbing." DEATH OF A LITTLE PRINCESS recounts the investigation into the horrifying murder of child beauty queen JonBenét Ramsey; the author is Don Davis, who wrote FALLEN HERO, the *New York Times* bestselling account of the O.J. Simpson case. Peter Meyer tells how a teenage love pact turned deadly in BLIND LOVE: *The True Story of the Texas Cadet Murders*. For those who believe slavery is a thing of the past, Wensley Clarkson proves them wrong in SLAVE GIRLS: *The Shocking World of Human Bondage*. Fannie Weinstein and Melinda Wilson tell the story of a beautiful honors student who was lured into the dark world of sex for hire in THE COED CALL GIRL MURDER.

St. Martin's True Crime Library gives you the stories *behind* the headlines. Our authors take you right to the scene of the crime and into the minds of the most notorious murderers to show you what really makes them tick. St. Martin's True Crime Library paperbacks are better than the most terrifying thriller, because it's all true! The next time you want a crackling good read, make sure it's got the St. Martin's True Crime Library logo on the spine—you'll be up all night!

Charles E. Spicer, Jr.
Senior Editor, St. Martin's True Crime Library

VICTOR TAKES ALL ...

The shotgun blast tore into Marty Dillon's chest, entering just above the sternum and instantly destroying his heart. Blood spattered on his clothes, the instep of his left boot, the ear protectors and sunglasses he wore and onto the tree stump beside him. Microscopic droplets expelled into the air at least five feet, far enough to settle onto the jeans and boots of Dr. Stephen Scher.

In the stillness of the Gunsmoke rifle-range, the body of Martin Thomas Dillon dropped face down on the ground, the clay pigeons falling from his hands. The echo of the gunshot blast faded and once again there was only silence.

Dr. Stephen Scher drew a sharp breath. Just weeks earlier, Patricia Dillon had ended their yearlong affair, after her husband had at last demanded she make a choice. And she had. She would stay in the marriage. She would stop seeing the doctor.

But now, in a moment, in the pull of a trigger, that decision had been reversed. Two lives collided in the blast of a shotgun. Now all that remained was for the victor to take all.

ALSO BY MARIA EFTIMIADES

LETHAL LOLITA
GARDEN OF GRAVES
MY NAME IS KATHERINE
SINS OF THE MOTHER

From St. Martin's Paperbacks

SECRETS
FROM THE
GRAVE

Maria Eftimiades

St. Martin's Paperbacks

SECRETS FROM THE GRAVE

Copyright © 1998 by Maria Eftimiades.

Cover photograph by Rich Banick/Gamma Liaison

ISBN: 0-312-96584-2

Printed in the United States of America

St. Martin's Paperbacks edition/May 1998

10 9 8 7 6 5 4 3 2 1

Acknowledgments

I am grateful to *People* Assistant Managing Editor Joe Treen for his deft edit of this manuscript, for his criticisms and suggestions, and for his support and interest in this project. I would also like to thank the many kind people I met in researching this book, especially those Montrose residents who shared their memories and anecdotes.

CHAPTER 1

A firm pull of the trigger, a blast, and the grasp releases, sending the clay pigeon tumbling to the ground, unbroken. In the shade of the skeet machine, the stillness of the woods kept score. Along the path that afternoon two sets of footprints marked the journey's start. By day's end, shadows darkened the retreating steps of only one.

There was a misty quiet at Gunsmoke that day, one only a man who had walked the woods as a boy could know. In the stillness was a whispered pledge, that the secrets of the forest are kept. But the forest would suppress the truth for only so long, for the paths taken by its visitors are recorded in every man's soul, and the soul must ultimately have its say. And the just man his day.

It was nearing noon on June 2, 1976, when attorney Martin Dillon and his client Kendall Strawn wrapped up a real estate closing at County Bank in Montrose, Pennsylvania, a quiet hilltop town amid the Endless Mountains in the northeastern tip of the state. For the thirty-year-old Dillon, the workday was almost over.

As had become his custom in recent years, Marty took off most Wednesday afternoons to skeet-shoot with friends on a plot of land his parents owned and affectionately called Gunsmoke, about twelve miles northwest of Montrose. At the camp, the members of "the Wednesday Afternoon Club," as Marty and his pals dubbed themselves, took turns shooting clay pigeons, with occasional breaks for beer and cigarettes.

Kendall Strawn didn't live in the area and wasn't part of the club, but he was a close friend, and today Marty Dillon wanted company. Leaning against Strawn's Jeep in the parking lot, the young lawyer tried to cajole the burly thirty-six-year-old developer into an afternoon at the Dillon camp.

"Come shoot with us," he urged Strawn. "Couple of hours up at Gunsmoke. Come on. It'll be fun."

Kendall Strawn wasn't tempted. His mind was racing with all he had to get done that afternoon. Lately, he'd been working seven days a week managing his properties, in addition to running the farm he owned in Le Raysville, west of Montrose. He barely found time to spend with his wife, Joan, and baby daughter, Tami.

"Marty, I just can't," he said apologetically. "I'm too busy."

Marty wasn't giving up. "What else do you have to do?" he pressed.

For a moment Kendall thought he detected a touch of urgency in his friend's voice, but then Marty smiled.

"You don't have anything to do," he told Kendall, teasing. "Come on, let's go shoot."

Three other friends, Marty explained, couldn't make it. Gary Passmore, an administrator at Montrose General Hospital, canceled that morning; it was his wife's birthday. Earle Wootton, publisher of the *Montrose Independent* newspaper, left a message saying he was too busy. And John Dabulewicz, an X-ray technician at the hospital, said he, too, had to pass.

That left Marty with just one member of the Wednesday Afternoon Club—Dr. Stephen Scher, an allergist at Montrose General.

Kendall Strawn grasped the situation at once, but since Marty didn't volunteer anything further he decided not to ask. In the past, when Kendall had offered his opinion, he'd gotten the impression that Marty didn't always appreciate his candor. And so now, when Dr. Stephen Scher's name was mentioned, Kendall tread cautiously. A husband's denial, he knew, was a powerful force.

After Kendall drove off, Marty Dillon headed to his law office at the top of Public Avenue, just a few doors away from the bank. Since he returned to his hometown after graduating from law school five years earlier, he'd landed a prime partnership with Robert Dean, one of the most respected attorneys in Susquehanna County. Marty's practice was particularly busy. Land prices in the area had begun rising in the early 1970s, and the local economy was thriving. Many chose to live in the town of two thousand lined with lakefront, hundred-year-old Victorian homes and commute to jobs in cities like Binghamton, New York, twenty miles north, or Scranton, Pennsylvania, thirty miles south. Marty handled as many as a dozen real estate closings a week while his criminal defense practice continued to grow.

At his desk that afternoon, Marty Dillon thumbed through motions for a homicide case in which he'd been appointed public defender. It was to be the young lawyer's first murder trial. His client was accused of beating a Choconut, Pennsylvania, man to death, and the evidence against him was compelling. It wasn't going to be easy.

Marty was having difficulty concentrating on the case. He'd been fighting the tension that had been building all day, ever since Gary Passmore called to say he couldn't make it to camp. Dillon's spirits rose once that day when his secretary, Bonnie Mead, told him he had a call from Anthony Amendola, an old friend who'd moved to Florida but was back in town for the week. Marty reached for the phone, relieved.

"What are you doing today?" he asked immediately.

Amendola explained he had a business meeting that afternoon and dinner plans in the evening.

Marty paid no attention. "We're going out to camp to do some shooting. Do you want to go?"

Amendola couldn't, and Marty's hopes dimmed. By now, there wasn't anyone left to ask.

In the quiet of his office, Marty Dillon pushed the swirling doubts from his mind, a technique he'd all but perfected in the past two years. As he left for Gunsmoke that June day, he stopped by Bonnie Mead's desk and told her and the other young women in the office a joke. Their laughter echoed in the back room as Marty pulled the front door closed behind him.

On the way to his car, Marty ran into Pennsylvania state troopers John Fekette and John Salinkas, and the three men chatted briefly about the murder trial. Then Marty got into his red BMW and headed just half a mile down Church Street, pulling into the driveway of number 85, a white, wooden two-family house across the street from Montrose General Hospital. Retrieving a change of clothes from the car, Marty Dillon climbed the front porch steps to the home of Dr. Stephen Scher.

The doctor stood in the doorway. In jeans, a blue and white striped long-sleeved shirt, and a brown jacket, the six-foot-one, 245-pound physician cast an imposing figure, his straight brown hair lightly framed in gray, his small, intense brown eyes shrouded behind wire-rimmed glasses. Although heavyset and somewhat unkempt in appearance, the thirty-six-year-old Scher exuded an almost militant self-assuredness. Some called it arrogance and did not much care for the doctor. But others in Montrose, particularly women, thought highly of Scher. Recently separated from his wife, Ann, the doctor kept an active social calendar.

Marty went inside to change out of his suit into brown corduroy pants, a blue shirt, tan leather vest, and brown boots. If he was uneasy in the doctor's home, he hid it aptly. He'd become quite skilled at that; he'd had plenty of practice. And today, like so many times before, it seemed easier to go along with the plans than to explain his reluctance: Marty Dillon was without a doubt a nonconfrontational man.

Besides, he reminded himself, the past didn't matter anymore. Just a week or so earlier, the ultimatum had been issued, the promise made. Marty had prevailed.

And so when he emerged from the house, even though Scher had already loaded the guns and ammunition into his own gray Ford and was seated in the driver's seat, Marty took his first step toward securing a different course in his relationship with Stephen Scher. The young lawyer motioned to his BMW. "We'll take my car," he called out to the doctor.

If the gesture appeared small, for Marty Dillon it was not. It was behind the wheel of his sports car that Marty was able to take control. It was what he loved about cars, maneuvering the curves, speeding along the hilly country roads he knew so well. He'd been in the passenger seat for too long. On June 2, 1976, Marty Dillon believed that had changed at last.

By three-thirty the BMW veered past the Susquehanna County Court of Common Pleas at the top of Public Avenue. After a quick stop at the Forest Lake Inn to pick up a six-pack of Pabst Blue Ribbon, the two men proceeded to Route 267 for the fifteen-minute drive to Silver Lake Township, eventually turning onto Russin Road, a dirt path up the mountain. As they sped past the modest white-shingled home of Andrew Russin, a sixty-five-year-old retired mechanical engineer, Marty beeped the horn once, and Russin, weeding in his garden, looked up and waved. The older man lived with his wife, Anna, and their twenty-one-year-old mentally disabled son, David, and kept an eye on Gunsmoke for the Dillons. In the past, Russin had trekked up to the property after he'd heard persistent shooting, assuming trespassers were hunting on the land: So now, when Marty visited he always let his neighbor know he was around.

Dr. Scher got out of the car to unfasten the cable on the gate at the entrance to the Dillon property, and the gravel on the dirt road flew as the BMW raced the final mile, pulling to a stop in front of a trailer surrounded by dense woods. The two men unloaded the car, bringing hamburger meat, ketchup, relish, bread, and chips into the makeshift kitchen for a barbecue that evening. The trailer was modestly furnished—mostly a place to rest, use the bathroom, and grab a cold beer.

They sat on the porch, opened beers, and smoked cigarettes. They talked about Marty's murder case: The young lawyer had questions about head injuries, and the doctor told him what he knew. They discussed Dr. Scher's upcoming trip to Knoxville with Gary Passmore to visit a mutual friend. Dillon and Scher agreed it was a good thing that Passmore had remembered his wife's birthday and skipped going to Gunsmoke that day.

Then the two men each put a beer in their jacket pockets and walked a couple of hundred feet up a wooded path to a clearing, carrying the guns, clay birds, and the skeet machine. Marty brought along his sunglasses and a pair of gray-and-black ear protectors. They set up the skeet at the edge of the field near a tree stump and for a short time took turns shooting ten birds each—first Scher, then Dillon. They each drank another beer, ate potato chips, and smoked some more. Marty preferred Winstons, the doctor, Marlboros.

It was just before six p.m.

At 7 Kelly Street in Montrose, Marty's two children waited for him to return home that evening. Suzanne would turn three in a few weeks. Five-year-old

Michael loved race cars, just like his dad.

And Pat, Marty's wife. A stunning woman, everyone said so. Pat was home, too, waiting for the man she loved.

Marty Dillon reached for the clay birds, holding one in each hand. His shirt caught the breeze, billowing slightly away from his body. His foot turned inward as he squatted by the machine. Wearing the gray-and-black ear protectors and sunglasses, he lowered his head. It was his turn to load the skeet.

Dr. Stephen Scher stood about four feet away. He reached for a number 4 shell; it was far more powerful than the number 8s they'd been using all day, the shells ordinarily used for skeet. He loaded his 16-gauge shotgun, cocked it, and took aim. It was his turn to fire.

CHAPTER 2

The shotgun blast tore into Marty Dillon's chest, entering just above the sternum and instantly destroying his heart. Blood spattered on his clothes, the instep of his left boot, the ear protectors and sunglasses he wore, and the tree stump beside him. Microscopic droplets were expelled into the air at least five feet, far enough to settle onto the jeans and boots of Dr. Stephen Scher.

In the stillness of Gunsmoke the body of Martin Thomas Dillon dropped facedown on the ground, the clay pigeons falling from his hands. The echo of the gunshot blast faded, and once again there was only silence.

Dr. Stephen Scher drew a sharp breath. Just weeks earlier, Patricia Dillon had ended their yearlong affair, after her husband had at last demanded that she make a choice. And she had. She would stay in the marriage. She would stop seeing the doctor.

But now, in a moment, in the pull of a trigger, that decision had been reversed. Two lives collided in the blast of a shotgun. Now all that remained was for the victor to take all.

In the mind of Dr. Stephen Scher, it was his due. He was, after all, a physician—a healer, they called him. He would now have the life he wanted, the life that had belonged to Martin Dillon.

It was by chance that Scher's opportunity arose: alone with Dillon, unexpectedly. A couple of beers for courage. A shotgun. A hurried plan. How effortlessly it came together, how natural it felt to step into another man's dreams.

But now, as the sun dipped lower into the Endless Mountains, a single focus emerged for Dr. Stephen Scher: self-preservation. Before the first telephone rang in Montrose, before state troopers arrived to cordon off the scene, the coroner was called, the families were notified, and the newspapers were alerted, the explanation must be ready. With the mistaken belief that the secrets of the forest were forever kept, the possibilities began to tick in the mind of Stephen Barry Scher.

With a single push, the doctor rolled the body of his rival onto its back. He laid down the 16-gauge Winchester several feet away, the muzzle pointed toward his victim's head. He bent over and untied Marty's right shoelace. As he prepared to leave, in his final moment alone at Gunsmoke, Stephen Scher reached into the young lawyer's pocket and removed his car keys.

This time, Scher would drive.

*   *   *

At first, Andrew Russin didn't recognize the tall, husky man at the door. The Russins didn't get too many visitors, living way up a dirt and gravel road in Silver Lake Township as they did. The older man had just quit gardening after his wife, Anna, called him in for supper. He hadn't heard the BMW pull into the driveway, just a sharp rap at the front windowpane.

"There was an accident and Marty's dead," the stranger said, his voice expressionless. "He was shot."

Russin swiftly made the connection. He'd met Dr. Scher once, not long ago, up at Gunsmoke when the Wednesday Club members were shooting skeet. Marty had been particularly upbeat that day, even inviting the older man to join the group. Russin was fond of the young attorney. The doctor's announcement was hard to believe.

"Are you sure he's dead?" he asked.

Scher nodded.

Russin noticed a ring of blood around the doctor's mouth. "What did you do, try to give him artificial respiration?" he asked.

Scher told him he had. Then he added that Russin needed to call for help.

As Scher waited in the kitchen, Andrew Russin phoned the Silver Lake Ambulance Squad and reported an accident at Gunsmoke. When he reappeared, Scher asked him to return with him to the Dillon property, and the older man agreed, beckoning to his son David to join them.

Before they left, Russin turned to Scher. "Do you want to wash up?" he asked. "There's a bathroom right here."

Scher refused. As the men began to leave, Anna

Russin stopped her husband at the door. "Here, take this," she said softly, holding out a worn blanket. "Cover him."

Russin and his son followed the BMW driven by Stephen Scher in Russin's 1966 white Jeep. About a half mile up the road, at the turn for Gunsmoke, Russin stopped and told David to get out and wait at the corner for the ambulance.

"Stand there," he explained carefully. "If someone comes, tell them which way to get to the Dillons'."

Andrew Russin proceeded about a mile and a half to the Dillon trailer and then followed the doctor by foot up the path. At first Russin could see only the soles of a pair of boots, but as he continued up the slight upgrade, the crumpled figure on the ground came into view.

The two men stood silently over the body.

"He fell on his gun," Dr. Scher said quietly. "He shot himself."

Andrew Russin nodded. He had no reason to question the doctor. Russin himself had been handling firearms since he was sixteen years old, growing up in nearby Carbondale, and he owned an extensive collection of rifles and pistols. He often told his children when they were small that he always assumed every gun was loaded. A man couldn't be too careful, he'd say. Accidents happen.

Russin took the blanket his wife had given him and began to cover the body. Stephen Scher walked behind him, and out of the corner of his eye, Russin saw him pick up the 16-gauge Winchester, lying in the shade of an ironwood tree.

As Andrew Russin watched in alarm, the doctor

lifted the gun by the muzzle, eased it back like a baseball bat, and with full force swung it directly at the ironwood.

."Don't!" Russin shouted.

It was too late. The gun smashed into the tree, breaking in two pieces, cracking the stock and sending it flying more than twenty feet away. Stephen Scher's voice, tinged with anger, boomed into the woods, splitting the melancholy quiet where the body lay. "This goddamn gun will never kill again!" he shouted.

An astonished Andrew Russin could only stare at the doctor. He sighed with relief that the gun had not discharged accidentally—for the second time that day.

At that point the first emergency medical technicians, Don and Susan Strope, arrived. It had been Susan Strope who'd taken Russin's call on the emergency phone installed in her home, and she had immediately broadcast over the Plekturn radio a request for rescue squad members to head to the scene.

She'd been preparing dinner when the call came in, so Susan Strope turned off the stove and hurried to her 1969 Mercury. She was heading out of the driveway when she ran into her husband, who was just arriving home from work. When she told him about the shooting accident he got into her car at once.

At Gunsmoke, Don Strope jumped out as his wife parked by the trailer, and he trotted up the path. When he reached the crest of the incline and saw the two men leaning over a body, one of them with his face and hands bloody, Strope quickly turned around and took a few steps down the trail, putting up his hand

and motioning to his wife, who was approaching, to stop. She did.

"Help this man," he called out to her, pointing to Stephen Scher.

The doctor walked along the trail toward Susan Strope and then turned and buried his face against a tree. He wrapped his arms around the trunk and began to cry.

Susan Strope waited for a moment, unsure of how to comfort the distraught man hugging the tree. She touched him gently on the shoulder and identified herself, explaining that she was with the rescue squad. She asked what she could do to help.

"I'm having chest pains," Stephen Scher said, gasping between sobs.

Concerned, Strope asked him if he had a heart condition and Scher nodded. When she asked if he had any nitroglycerine pills, the tearful man told her he'd already taken two.

"I'm a doctor," he explained. "I'm Dr. Scher."

Susan Strope had heard the name but had never met Scher. She led him to her car and motioned for him to sit in the passenger seat. She rummaged through her first aid bag and handed him a moist towelette.

"Why don't you wipe the blood off your mouth and hands?" Strope suggested kindly.

By now, John Conarton, the Susquehanna County coroner, had pulled up to the trailer. Conarton had received a call from the county commissioner minutes after the radio call was first broadcast and headed over at once.

When he saw the coroner, Stephen Scher began to weep again. "My best friend," he moaned. "I can't believe he's dead. He was my best friend."

Choking back sobs, Stephen Scher told Conarton about the accident. Marty had been running with the Winchester and he fell. He must have tripped over some root on the ground. And the gun discharged.

"He was my best friend," Scher repeated between sobs.

John Conarton listened sympathetically. He knew Dr. Scher from the hospital. A good man, he'd always thought, a respected physician. As far as he was concerned, there was no need for more questions, no point for further investigation.

Indeed, less than an hour after Stephen Scher shot Martin Dillon at Gunsmoke, the doctor happened upon extraordinary good fortune: His words and tears were enough for John Conarton. The coroner was sold.

Over the next half hour a handful of other officials arrived on the scene. Bob Elliott, a part-time game commissioner, was among the first. He'd heard the emergency radio call go out and immediately summoned a deputy, Jerry Thorne, and then proceeded to Gunsmoke from his house on Laurel Lake, about four miles away. A short time later, Conarton walked down to the intersection to meet the first Pennsylvania state trooper on the scene, William Hairston, and guide him to the Dillons' property. Hairston had received a radio call at his base, Troop R in Dunmore, and responded immediately, arriving at about seven-thirty.

The moment the two men met on the path, John Conarton unequivocally stated what he'd learned in his few minutes at Gunsmoke, exactly what Dr. Scher had told him. "It is an accidental shooting," the coroner said.

Hairston did not object to the coroner's pronouncement. The trooper was a rookie—he'd never even been to the scene of a shooting death before. As he followed Conarton up the trail, Hairston learned that the distraught man sitting in the Stropes' car was Dr. Stephen Scher, the only other person at Gunsmoke at the time of the shooting. The coroner told him it was all quite simple: Dillon tripped. He fell and shot himself in the chest. An accident. It was an accident.

At the scene, Hairston assumed jurisdiction for the Pennsylvania state police, taking over from the game wardens, and cordoned off the area. He walked around the body. He saw the black-and-gray ear protectors and a pair of sunglasses streaked with blood lying a few yards away. He observed the broken Winchester, the pump handle six feet from the body; the stock another twenty-five feet away. Nearby, he could see a tree stump spattered with blood, with a second firearm, a double-barreled shotgun, on top, with no rounds in either barrel. He noticed the blood on Dillon's shoe. He observed that the lawyer's right shoelace was untied.

Hairston asked Bob Elliott to clear the chamber of the Winchester, and the game warden did, removing the number 4 shot expended cartridge from the barrel and a number 8 shot unexpended cartridge from the magazine. Elliot then began to search the path for any protruding roots Marty might have stumbled on.

Hairston and Conarton walked back to the trailer. The trooper asked Scher to follow him to his police car, and the doctor did, getting into the passenger seat. Hairston and the coroner climbed into the backseat, and the trooper pulled out a pen and pad of paper.

"What happened?" he asked Scher.

The doctor began to speak. Hairston scribbled notes, writing in the first person, keeping up as best he could.

"We came up to do some skeet shooting," Scher told him. "We had shot about 20 rounds and decided to take a breather. We went back to the trailer to get some more beer. Marty had some potato chips. We sat around for a while, talking about an upcoming murder trial. We got some more rounds and went back up the trail. We shot a couple more rounds and Marty wanted to go back to the trailer to get his cigarettes. I loaded my shotgun so I'd be ready for the next round. Marty unloaded his and set it on the stump. We started walking down the trail and I laid my gun on the stand you passed coming down the trail. As we went a little farther Marty turned around and said he saw something in the open field and that it might be the porcupine his dad had been after. He then told me to keep my eye on it and he ran up the trail and grabbed my gun from the stand. I heard him cock it, then I heard the gun go off. I yelled to him, 'What the hell are you shooting at? You missed him.' But I couldn't see him from where I was. So I go up the path and I saw him lying on the ground face down. I ran up to him and turned him over and saw him bleeding from the chest. I tried to stop it but I couldn't. I gave him mouth to mouth but I knew he was dead."

Scher turned to John Conarton, who was nodding understandingly. "John, I'm a doctor," he said. "I knew he was dead. Then I turned and started running down the trail and I started to get chest pains so I turned around and went back to get the car keys out of Marty's pocket. I then drove to Russin's place and told him what happened. Me and Russin came back and I took him where Marty was. I looked down and saw the gun and picked it up and said, 'the goddamn trigger got a twig in it' and at the same time smashed it against the tree. I know I shouldn't have done that.''

It was done: Stephen Scher's first words to authorities describing the tragic, bizarre accident to befall Martin Dillon in the woods of Gunsmoke. It was an account that would ring hollow for those who understood guns and the trajectory of bullets, for those schooled in examining blood spatter and crime scenes. But mostly, the story of the porcupine in the woods at Gunsmoke, of Dillon snatching the doctor's Winchester off the stand and running with a loaded gun, of Scher, his back turned, walking down the path to the trailer would immediately arouse suspicion in those who knew Stephen Scher and Martin Dillon. And in the days that followed, as the doctor was forced to repeat his account of that evening to friends, family, and officials, the facts would change, in the smallest of details, in the subtlest of ways, as lies tend to do. It would fuel the belief in many that something very different occurred on June 2, 1976.

But now, as dusk fell, Trooper Hairston offered no reaction to what he'd just heard and asked no further questions. He simply folded the paper with Scher's explanation, put it into his pocket, and got out of the car. He soon received a radio call to meet Frank Zanin, the records and identification officer from Gibson Barracks, at the entrance to Gunsmoke and to lead him to the scene. For the next hour or so, Hairston, the coroner, and game wardens continued to walk back and forth, from the body to the trailer, taking measurements and photographs, talking in low voices.

Stephen Scher waited quietly by the cars. While the authorities were up at the clearing, the doctor could relax. After all, he believed he was shielded from judgmental eyes.

He was wrong.

Carol Gazda was watching. The volunteer first aid technician had been seated in her 1969 Chevelle parked a few yards away from Scher for more than an hour; in fact, she'd arrived shortly after the Stropes. She'd heard the call over the Plekturn radio and immediately headed over, taking along her five-year-old daughter, Cindy.

But when Carol Gazda got to Gunsmoke and began walking up the path, she saw that her husband Tom was already on the scene. He caught sight of her and frantically waved her away. "Out of here now with her!" he shouted, pointing to Cindy. "Turn around. Go! Right now! I don't want her to see this!"

And so Carol had grabbed her daughter's hand and led her back to the car. And it was there that she waited. She had no idea what was going on. She didn't know who any of these people were. Carol had never met Marty Dillon. She'd never heard of Stephen Scher.

She did not know that he was the man who stood in front of her, alternately leaning against the Stropes' car and walking around it. But she could hardly take her eyes off him.

Because over and over, Carol Gazda watched behavior she could hardly believe. A man sitting quietly, looking as if nothing was wrong, placid and calm. Then someone would appear from inside the trailer or up the path. A trooper, the coroner, an EMT worker. And the man in front of her, as if on cue, would suddenly begin to cry. "My best friend," he'd sob. "He was my best friend."

For a little more than an hour, Carol Gazda watched Stephen Scher turn off and on half a dozen times, calm in his solitude, breaking down the moment anyone approached.

"I can't believe it," he'd sob. "I can't believe my best friend is dead."

It was the strangest sight Carol Gazda had ever observed. She felt as if she were invisible, the only witness to this inexplicable scene. For some reason, Stephen Scher didn't notice her sitting quietly in her car.

She had no idea what she was seeing. She only knew something felt terribly wrong. Who is this guy? she thought.

CHAPTER 3

In Montrose in 1976, the answer varied greatly. To some, Stephen Scher was the consummate compassionate physician who made house calls without complaint and cared about his patients. His admirers responded to his quick wit, his gentle, soft-spoken manner, the way he listened intently.

To others he showed a different side, one critical and cold, a man who had affairs with wives of friends, a doctor who was quick to shift blame for mistakes to the nursing staff, an arrogant opportunist who boasted that he always got what he wanted.

By all accounts, however, Stephen Scher had charm, an ability to take people in, to gain their trust. The only disagreement between his friends and detractors was whether it was genuine.

Stephen Barry Scher was born on May 10, 1940, to Jewish parents in Toronto, Canada. His sister, Susan, is two and a half years younger than he is. When he was eight, his family relocated to Florida for his father's job, selling baby clothes. But three years later, out of town on a business trip, Scher's father, in his early forties, died of a massive heart attack.

The death hit the family hard. The Schers moved into a smaller apartment and young Stephen began to work after school. Within two years, there were more major adjustments to make. His mother remarried, and now he had not only a new stepfather but also two stepbrothers.

For as long as he could remember, Stephen Scher wanted to become a doctor, and following his father's death, his determination only increased. He earned good grades in high school, and became a naturalized U.S. citizen at age sixteen. He enrolled at the University of Miami, intending to be a premed student. But a month after school began, in October 1958, Stephen Scher's mother died of breast cancer. Without other family members in the area, he and his sister left Florida; Susan went to live with an aunt in Toronto, and Stephen transferred his credits to the University of Michigan, moving in with his father's brother, who lived near Ann Arbor.

It was a difficult time for Stephen Scher. Losing his parents so young left him feeling adrift in the world, unsure of whom to trust. He worried about making it through school and achieving the goals he'd set for himself. With few friends and almost no money, Scher immersed himself in his schoolwork.

Then one night in 1960 he went to a university dance and met Edna Ann Elias, a botany and bacteriology student with whom he shared some science courses. They began to date and quickly became an item around campus. In 1962, Scher was accepted at the university's medical school. A year later, on June 9, 1963, he and Ann, both twenty-three years old, were married in a Jewish ceremony in the town of Milan, about twenty miles south.

The young couple rented a farm on the outskirts of Ann Arbor, and Ann paid the bills by working at the university hospital as a microbiologist. Scher helped out too, working part-time at the same clinic, earning fifty cents an hour to be on call every other night and weekends. In the early years of the marriage, Ann became interested in raising purebred dogs. Her new husband encouraged her, installing a kennel on the farm.

When Stephen Scher graduated medical school in May 1965, the couple remained at the farm while he did his internship in nearby Dearborn. A year later, with tensions mounting in Vietnam, Scher opted to complete his residency requirements through the United States Public Health Service in lieu of military service.

Stephen Scher was placed at the Laguna Indian Reservation about fifty miles west of Albuquerque, and for the next two years he served as a public health officer, caring for some ten thousand Navajo and Pueblo Indians with one other physician. Because of their dogs, the Schers couldn't live in government housing, so they rented land and a trailer on the reservation and set up a kennel. The young couple had no television and no phone. But these were good years, a period of building and planning their future together.

During Scher's second year on the reservation, he and Ann started to consider job offers in small communities where he could build a family practice. Both preferred to live in the country, and they also agreed to focus only on the East Coast, due to the proximity of cities that hosted the more prestigious dog shows. By now, Ann Scher was showing several of their dogs.

The couple pored through real estate brochures and offers from various hospitals and narrowed their scope to eight. Finally, they picked one.

In July 1968, they moved to Montrose, Pennsylvania.

With a two-year contract and a guaranteed income from Montrose General Hospital's Medical Arts Clinic, the Schers bought a 175-acre farm for $35,000 on the periphery of town, with two Scotch-Irish heifers, Newfoundland dogs, and chickens. They later purchased a two-family house at 85 Church Street as an investment property.

For those first few years, Ann dropped in to the clinic frequently to visit her husband and worked twice a week with him in his office. The couple shared a common interest in medicine and often discussed the latest journals together. Two years after they moved to the area, Scher took over another physician's practice in New Milford, about nine miles away, after the physician was diagnosed with cancer. With two practices growing, Stephen Scher worked long hours, making house calls in the mornings, staying late into the evening at the office. His reputation was mixed—some found him curt and distant, others liked him—but all concurred that he was devoted to medicine.

Then, in 1971, at the age of thirty-one, Stephen Scher suffered a heart attack. He spent three weeks recovering in Montrose General. Once he was released and could return to work, hospital administrators took him off night duty rotation so he could sleep uninterrupted.

It was following that incident that Ann Scher gradually noticed changes in her husband. He lost weight and stopped smoking. He began to avoid having sex with her; she believed he was afraid of triggering another heart attack. He talked often about his belief that he would die young, like his parents. He was sure he would be dead by age forty-five, he told his wife.

Ann believed that in reaction to his fear Stephen Scher began to focus solely on himself, his needs and desires. She later told friends it was as if he'd made the decision that he was going to do whatever he wanted to do. In many ways, it fit the pattern of his early years when he suffered the loss of his parents and learned to depend only on himself. It was as if somewhere along life's path, Stephen Scher took a dangerous turn, trusting no one, respecting only his own ambition and the goals he set out to achieve. And now, having at last met his objective of becoming a physician and gaining the veneration of others, Stephen Scher, newly aware of his mortality, was going to make sure he missed out on nothing.

Perhaps there were seeds of such a personality all along, Ann thought years later. She was well aware that her husband was a master at controlling situations, at manipulating people and ensuring that he was never on the losing side. From the early days of their marriage, she also knew that he had frequent mood swings, turning aloof and cold with no explanation. He never was a generous man; indeed, his tightness with money had become an issue in the marriage. Ann came to dread her husband's constant haggling over dividing checks when they went out with others and hearing his complaints later about getting short-changed.

But in the early 1970s, Stephen Scher began to treat her with a derisiveness that stunned her, a disregard that gradually chipped away at her self-esteem. He told her not to stop at the clinic anymore. He often left on weekends to go bowling or to play golf and said nothing to her—he'd just go. Some nights he didn't come home at all, showing up in the early morning hours refusing to explain where he'd been.

From time to time, Ann Scher attempted to broach a discussion about the changes in their relationship. He always dismissed her sharply. "Don't aggravate me," he'd say. "You're making me have chest pains."

For a while, Ann Scher held out hope that her marriage might be saved. She hadn't been able to become pregnant, although at one time the couple talked about adopting a child. But as Scher continued to spend time away from home, leaving the responsibility of the farm to her, Ann wondered what life would be like if they were parents.

One day, she gave him a hypothetical. "If we were going to Bermuda and the baby got sick, what would happen?" she asked.

Scher didn't hesitate. "You'd stay home," he answered nonchalantly, "and I'd go."

As the distance between them grew, Ann slowly sank into a depression, furthering the collapse of the relationship. Scher occasionally brought her sedatives and antidepressants from the hospital, but nothing seemed to help—some mornings Ann had trouble getting out of bed. Stephen Scher complained that the house was untidy, that he couldn't stand the dogs and their paraphernalia in practically every room. The marriage was clearly in deep trouble.

Then, in the fall of 1971, Pat Dillon joined the nursing staff at Montrose General.

She was Patty Dillon then, slight and dark-haired, with a soft voice and warm brown eyes. She had just returned to the area with her husband and their infant son after spending several years in the Philadelphia area. Taking a job at Montrose General felt comfortable for Patty—she'd worked in the clinic a few summers before and had even gone to Dr. Stephen Scher as a patient. In fact, it had been Scher who'd confirmed her pregnancy with her son Michael.

She'd grown up Patricia Rosalie Karveller, the adored daughter of John, a popular math teacher at the high school, and Laura, a devoted homemaker who was known as a fabulous cook. Patty was an only child until she was twelve, when her parents adopted a son, Robby. The Karvellers, Italian and Polish, were staunch Catholics who attended church regularly and lived in a rambling white-shingled corner house with a big barn on Chenango Street, down the block from the Susquehanna County courthouse in the center of town. Although the neighborhood was filled with children, Patty Karveller seldom played with them, only on rare occasions joining their hide-and-seek games on summer nights or sleigh riding in the park on winter afternoons. She had a small circle of friends and spent most of her time with her closest friend, Kathy Novitske. Around the neighborhood it was well-known that Patty was infinitely spoiled by her parents. Indeed, her nickname was "Laura's little princess."

As she grew into adolescence, Patty continued to

distance herself from many of the young people in Montrose. They, in turn, considered her a snob and felt she looked down on them. At the same time, even her detractors couldn't help but marvel at Patty Karveller. As a teenager, she was stunning and poised, with a buxom figure and long brown hair flipped at the ends, reminiscent of Annette Funicello.

Patty seemed to have it all. At Montrose Consolidated High School, she earned good grades, played flute and piano, and was a cheerleader and a soprano who sang solos in the church choir, even volunteering to sing seven o'clock mass in Latin several mornings a week.

Her confidence was almost daunting. Once in high school when the music teacher stopped the chorus and told Patty she was singing flat, she dismissed him with aplomb. "There's no way I'm singing flat," she announced.

Her classmates tittered as the teacher actually played back a tape in order to convince Patty.

The year before she graduated when she attended the junior prom with her boyfriend, Larry Allen, she was remembered as the only girl other than the prom queen to wear a tiara.

It was her mother who encouraged Patty to study nursing. That was the way Laura Karveller hoped her daughter would find a husband. Not just any man— a doctor. Indeed, Laura Karveller's plan for Patty was no secret.

She spoke so often about Patty marrying a doctor that friends described Laura Karveller as a firm believer in the adage, "It's just as easy to love a rich man as a poor man." Nothing, it seemed, was good enough for her daughter.

After graduating from high school in 1965, Patty joined her friend Kathy Novitske at the University of Pennsylvania School of Nursing, in Philadelphia. But Patty didn't fall in love with a medical student. She began to date Marty Dillon, whom she'd known casually from high school where he'd been one grade ahead of her. Their courtship quickly became serious, surprising their friends and family.

It wasn't what Laura Karveller had planned, but she liked Marty Dillon. He was handsome and ambitious. A placid and thoughtful young man with a dry sense of humor, Marty Dillon had dreams of becoming a renowned trial lawyer.

Martin Thomas Dillon was born to Lawrence Dillon, a shipyard worker, and his wife Josephine, on May 11, 1946, in Wilmington, Delaware. Larry Dillon had previously served as a medic in World War II.

After the birth of their son, the Dillons moved to Montrose, not far from the farm in northern Susquehanna County where Larry grew up. In town, Larry Dillon sold cars, delivered gasoline, and performed other odd jobs. Two years after Marty's birth, the Dillons had a daughter, Joann.

The Dillons didn't have a lot of money, but they were a tight-knit family and enjoyed spending time together. Larry Dillon's father had died when he was a child, and he was thrilled to have a son to carry on the Dillon name. From early childhood, father and son were the best of friends. Larry taught the boy to hunt, always stressing safety first. Young Marty took the lessons seriously.

Marty and his sister were also close. The two loved to swim at Forest Lake, where the Dillons occasionally stayed at a cottage owned by Jo's cousins, the Nashes. In high school, Marty played basketball and trombone in the band and was elected class president. After school he worked for Dave Andre at the local Agway, stocking shelves and sweeping the floors. On weekends he worked for Andre at home, helping the store owner put in stone walls and grating.

Marty's passion was always cars, fast cars. After school, he loved drag racing with his friends on a marked quarter mile outside town. He and his high school girlfriend, Joyce Wilcox, occasionally went to Binghamton, New York, to watch NASCAR races; often Larry and Jo Dillon joined them. Even when he was a teenager, Marty wasn't uncomfortable spending time with his family—indeed, he preferred it. Some of his Saturday night dates with Joyce were spent in the Dillon kitchen, helping his grandmother bake cookies.

In his senior year of high school, Marty participated in a year abroad program sponsored by the local Rotary, studying in Germany. His absence was felt keenly by the Dillons. When he returned, Marty graduated near the top of the 1964 senior class, and the school yearbook devoted an entire page to his adventure overseas.

The following fall, when Marty enrolled at Villanova University near Philadelphia, his parents were extremely proud. He worked hard and set his sights on law school. When he and Patty became serious, the Dillons were delighted. Joann, too, was happy, and she and Patty quickly became close. Joann had always wanted a sister, and now she had one.

Marty and Patty were married at Holy Name of Mary Church on August 31, 1968, a week before

Marty entered Villanova Law School. It was a big wedding—they even had a papal blessing. Patty had seven or eight bridesmaids, two flower girls, and two ring bearers. Her maid of honor was Kathy Novitske. Marty's ex-girlfriend, Joyce Wilcox, and his sister, Joann, were bridesmaids.

At the end of the aisle, amid the smiles of their families, the couple exchanged wedding bands. On Marty's, Pat had inscribed *PRK to MTD 8/31/68*. At the reception, held in Binghamton, they danced in each other's arms, radiantly happy.

The newlyweds settled into a modest apartment in Philadelphia while Marty attended law school and Pat took a nursing job at nearby Lankeau Hospital. Not long after the wedding, Marty's lifelong back pain became so troublesome that he underwent spinal surgery, but his new wife was supportive and helped him through it.

The early years of the Dillon marriage seemed ideal. They occasionally socialized with Joyce Wilcox and her new husband, Tom Jagger. Since neither couple had much money, they'd go to each other's apartments for popcorn and soda. At the hospital, Pat became friendly with Sue Graham, a nurse whose husband, Kerry, was in the air force. When Kerry Graham returned from overseas, he and Marty instantly hit it off, becoming close friends.

On occasional weekends, the couple traveled home to Montrose to visit their families. Patty served as maid of honor when her sister-in-law Joann married Alan Reimel in 1969. The following year, Patty became pregnant, and in January 1971, at the start of Marty's last semester of law school, the Dillons' first child, Michael, was born. A few months later, when

Marty graduated, the young family moved back to Montrose.

Marty was delighted to be home. He loved the woods and lakes of Susquehanna County and preferred to be closer to his family. Patty, too, was glad to be nearer to her own parents, especially with a new baby, but at the same time she felt a bit pressured by the proximity to her in-laws. Although Larry and Jo Dillon were always kind to her, Patty was somewhat threatened by their relationship with Marty. At times she complained that her husband seemed to put them first, ahead of her.

A year after they moved back home, the young couple bought a three-bedroom ranch at 7 Kelly Street for $24,000, just two doors away from Joann and Alan Reimel in a new development atop a hill a half mile from town. They faithfully attended Holy Name of Mary on Sundays with their families, and Marty joined the area Lions Club, eventually becoming its president. Marty also formed a racing club. In fact, he and Kendall Strawn were such avid fans of the sport they pooled their money to buy a race car, hiring a professional driver and occasionally taking weekend trips to watch him compete. Although Patty didn't care for racing, she gamely went along with Marty and their friends, Bob and Sue Caterson, to Watkins Glen for a race, staying overnight in a camper.

Marty put in long hours at Bob Dean's law firm. In the evenings, he often dropped by the Montrose Inn to hang out with his friends and drink. It seemed to him he had it all—a beautiful wife, an adorable son, a promising future.

At first, Patty seemed to be finding her niche as well, immersing herself into establishing their social status in town, arranging dinner parties and making contacts with affluent, established young couples. She also took a part-time nursing job at Montrose General. She was qualified to teach childbirth classes, and in the early 1970s, Lamaze was newly in vogue.

But before long, something seemed to be missing for Patty. Marty was busy all the time, distracted by work, his relationship with his parents, his interest in racing. He did not dote on her the way she had grown up believing a man would. And though she tried to fight it at first, she found herself becoming more attracted to a man who did.

At first, Patty Dillon and Dr. Stephen Scher were merely friends. Scher met Marty, and for a time the two men seemed to hit it off. When Marty refurbished the basement into a recreation room, Stephen Scher stopped by to help. But by the fall of 1972, nurses at Montrose General had noticed mild flirting and huddled conversations between Stephen Scher and Patty Dillon. At Hanukkah that year, Patty brought him a gift every day for eight days, surprising the hospital staff. By then, she was expecting her second child. As the pregnancy progressed, nurses observed how Dr. Scher seemed practically to follow Patty Dillon around the hospital.

Scher started to drop by the house in the mornings, after Marty had left for the office, to have coffee with Pat. Marty went along with Pat's suggestion that they socialize with the Schers as couples, going to minor league hockey games in Binghamton or to dinner at the Montrose Inn. Marty appeared not to notice that when the foursome was together it seemed as if Steve and Patty were the couple, sitting side by side, whispering and laughing together.

Ann Scher, however, did notice, and she didn't like it. From the start, she accused her husband of an affair with the nurse. He angrily denied it. "You're imagining things. I'm friends with both of the Dillons. There isn't anything between me and Pat."

At that point, Ann Scher was wrong—the affair wasn't yet physical—but the emotional bond between her husband and the young nurse was unmistakable, and it was growing steadily. In her despair, Ann Scher lashed out at her husband, who by then was all but ignoring her. Occasionally, though, he enjoyed dropping remarks to fuel her jealousy and to hint at his increasing role as an almost surrogate father to little Michael Dillon—he'd mention that he was helping Patty potty train the boy, or that they were taking him to learn to ice skate. Powerless to halt the inevitable, Ann sank deeper into depression. As for Scher, he continued progressively to insinuate himself into Marty Dillon's family.

It was never clearer to those at Montrose General than in late June 1973, when Patty Dillon gave birth to a daughter in a Wilkes-Barre hospital, about an hour and a half south of Montrose. Pat had chosen the hospital because a doctor there specialized in natural childbirth. When word of the birth of Suzanne Dillon reached Montrose General, Dr. Stephen Scher immediately announced that he had to go and see the baby. "I'm her pediatrician," he told the nurses as he practically ran out of the hospital.

Jo Ann Warner, the receptionist and switchboard operator that night, couldn't contain her amazement. The hospital was filled with patients, and the only doctor on duty had simply walked out.

"Is this a normal, healthy baby?" she asked nurses.

When told the child was fine, Jo Ann shook her head. She'd been observing the relationship between Stephen Scher and Patty Dillon and didn't like what she saw. She didn't care for Scher—she found him pompous—but she kept her feelings to herself. She was aware that Scher hadn't liked another receptionist and refused to allow the young woman to work while he was on duty. Before long, the receptionist couldn't get enough hours into her schedule and had to look for another job.

Jo Ann wasn't particularly fond of Patty either. They had grown up next door to each other on Chenango Street. Jo Ann saw Patty as a grown woman the same way as she'd been as a child—cordial, pleasant, but someone who thought she was a little better than everyone else.

Jo Ann and many of the nurses shared their disbelief about the relationship developing between Dr. Scher and Patty Dillon. The doctor didn't exactly take pains with his appearance. He was overweight and dressed sloppily. Nurses whispered about his body odor and dirty fingernails. Jo Ann couldn't understand it.

Marty's such a hunk, she often thought, and Dr. Scher is so unattractive. What does she see in him?

Perhaps Patty Dillon saw in Stephen Scher the image her mother spoke of throughout her childhood—the man people looked up to by virtue of his profession, a doctor, a healer. It was, after all, supposed to have been her future—the pampered child on Chenango Street, the talented teenager who turned heads, the helping nurse, and ultimately the doctor's wife.

But more important, Patty Dillon clearly received

something else from Stephen Scher—the attention she craved, the adoration she was given as a child.

She was headed down a dangerous path. And Marty Dillon refused to see what was happening.

CHAPTER 4

By 1974, Dr. Stephen Scher was arranging Pat's schedule so that they worked the same shifts. When he was on call, he'd leave Jo Ann Warner a phone number where he could be reached. At first, the receptionist didn't know whose number it was. Then she called one day and recognized Pat Dillon's voice.

The whispers about Scher and Pat Dillon were all over the hospital. Ann Scher was hearing the rumors, too, and she began to check up on her husband. It didn't take long to discover his lies. He'd say he was going to Syracuse for a medical meeting for the day, and Ann could see by the odometer on this car that he hadn't been anywhere. He'd tell her he was going on house calls, and she'd drive by the Dillons' and see his gray Ford in the driveway.

One Sunday when Scher told her he was working at the clinic, Ann phoned and asked to speak to him.

Jo Ann Warner took the call. Ordinarily, the young receptionist patched calls from wives directly to the doctors, and so when Ann Scher called, Warner simply told her the phone number Scher had given where he could be reached.

Ann Scher recognized the Dillons' number. She'd prepared lunch for her husband that day, and he'd never shown up. Furious, Ann drove to the clinic and waited in the parking lot. Word traveled throughout the hospital that an altercation was brewing, and indeed, when Scher's car finally pulled in, the windows all over Montrose General went up as the nurses listened to Ann Scher bitterly confront her husband.

On Christmas in 1974, Pat Dillon invited the Schers to join her and Marty at her parents' home for dinner. By now, Ann found it increasingly difficult to be around the young nurse. That night was no exception.

As the children played with their new toys, the conversation turned to Pat's education. Laura Karveller poured coffee and unabashedly talked about the plans the family had made for their daughter. "We sent Pat to nursing school and hoped she would marry a doctor," she said.

Karveller's casual announcement was greeted by silence. Ann felt sick. She looked at her husband and Pat and wondered what Marty Dillon was thinking. She couldn't wait to leave.

In early 1975, Stephen Scher decided to specialize in allergy, and he asked Pat to be his nurse. It was around that time that the two finally consummated their relationship. For almost three years their love affair had been chaste, yet the disloyalty to their spouses seemed just as real as if the relationship had been sexual. Now, the last step had been taken. The betrayal was complete.

Once they were having a sexual relationship, their behavior became even more obvious, like teenagers in love who couldn't get enough of each other. The chemistry between the doctor and nurse was unmistakable; the sparks that had been building were practically exploding.

Still, Marty Dillon refused to face the truth. He put in even longer hours at the office and began spending more time going to races on weekends and drinking at the Montrose Inn. He knew there was something wrong, but at the same time he couldn't imagine Patty unfaithful to him—Patty who went to church every Sunday, the mother of his two kids. His own sister lived just two doors away. Surely his wife couldn't be conducting an affair right there on Kelly Street.

At the same time, Marty Dillon was just as confused by Dr. Scher's behavior. He couldn't believe that Stephen Scher, who called him for lunch, dropped by his office to chat, and joined him skeet shooting, could be sleeping with his wife. It simply made no sense to him.

Marty's friend Kendall Strawn had no trouble seeing what Dillon could not. Strawn's curiosity about Pat Dillon and Dr. Stephen Scher had been piqued early on, when Marty mentioned casually that his wife and the doctor were planning to go to a medical conference out of town.

Something's funny about that, Kendall thought.

But since Marty didn't seem concerned, Kendall shrugged it off. Perhaps he was a bit too cynical, he thought.

Doc Scher's probably an old guy—sixty, seventy

years old, he decided. Patty must just be furthering
her education.

When Strawn finally met Stephen Scher, he was
taken aback to find a rather commanding man in his
mid-thirties. Strawn's suspicion increased in the winter of 1975, when Pat called him at his farm in Le
Raysville and encouraged him to go with Marty to a
race in Florida.

Kendall hesitated—he hadn't taken a vacation in
years—but Pat Dillon was persistent. Kendall finally
agreed, making plans with Marty to spend five days
in Tampa.

On the morning they were leaving, Marty told him
that Pat's back was bothering her and Dr. Scher had
dropped by the house to put her in traction.

Kendall Strawn didn't buy it. At the Dillon house
he purposely sought out Pat and asked her about her
back. She seemed nervous, refusing to catch his eye,
stumbling on her words. He knew she was lying. He
wondered if Marty realized it too.

On the trip, Kendall tried to feel him out. "Marty,
don't you think it's little strange that when you go
out of town Doc Scher has a reason to be at your
house?" he asked.

Marty didn't answer, and Kendall didn't pursue it.
It was not his place, he decided, to force a man to
see what he obviously didn't want to.

Kendall reminded himself of that again, when over
the next few months he and his wife, Joan, spent a
good deal of time with Pat Dillon and Stephen Scher
when they helped the Strawns adopt a baby girl from
a local teenager. The casual touching and chemistry
between the couple unsettled Strawn. The bond is so

strong, he thought. He wondered how Marty could stand it.

At the hospital, Jo Ann Warner wondered, too. Marty, she knew, had grown up in a very traditional household in which his mother catered to his father. Jo Ann always marveled at the relationship between the elder Dillons, how at buffet dinners in town Josephine always got up and fixed Larry's plate. It was cute to watch them together, Jo Ann often thought.

But knowing Patty as she did, Jo Ann suspected that maybe Marty Dillon had unrealistic expectations. Patty isn't fixing anyone's plate, Jo Ann mused.

Indeed, Jo Ann knew Patty well enough from childhood to realize how she craved attention.

And so when she saw Scher teasing and flirting with Patty she said to herself: He knows what buttons to push. She likes all this attention.

In the spring of 1975, with the full-blown affair underway for several months, Stephen Scher and Pat Dillon told their spouses they were going to an allergy conference in Canada. Marty Dillon helped load his wife's suitcase into Stephen Scher's car. If he suspected that anything was amiss, he didn't show it.

But Ann Scher did. She begged her husband not to go. She confronted him with what she'd been hearing, about all the time he'd been spending with the young nurse. She pleaded with him to give their relationship another chance. "Don't replace me with Pat," she sobbed. "Please don't go with her. We could work together like we used to. Take me. Please take me."

Stephen Scher did not answer and continued to pack for the trip. As his wife became almost hysterical, he walked out. Later that day, in the bathroom,

Ann found a vial of about forty yellow capsules of Nembutal. She'd never seen them in the house before. She didn't take the pills, but she believed in her heart that her husband left them in the hope she would. He wants me to make it easy for him, she thought in her despair.

Ann Scher cried her way through the weekend. Meanwhile, in Canada, her husband took Pat to meet some of his relatives in a Toronto suburb.

The end of the Scher's marriage was approaching. In July the Schers and the Dillons went to a resort in Wyoming where Pat and Steve were to attend an allergy seminar. Perhaps mindful of taking too many trips alone together, this time it was to be as a foursome.

Before they left Montrose, Ann Scher summoned her courage and asked her husband what she'd been wanting to for months: if he was in love with Pat Dillon.

"I don't know," he answered.

They flew to Wyoming with the Dillons. Shortly after they arrived, Pat and Steve left to take a class, and Ann decided to go for a swim. She was halfway across the lawn when she ran into Marty Dillon.

"Where are you going?" he asked.

"To the pool. I need to blow off some steam and get some exercise."

Marty Dillon looked at her sadly. "Don't go over there," he warned softly.

Ann went anyway. She quickly saw what Marty had just witnessed: her husband and his wife reclining on beach chairs by the pool. Stephen Scher was massaging Pat's legs.

Ann hurried back across the grass. Marty was waiting.

"Come with me," he said. "I'll buy you a drink."

"No," she said, breaking into tears. "Just leave me alone."

Marty told her that he wanted to return to Montrose. "I'm trying to get different plane reservations, but I haven't been able to get them switched. I want to get Pat out of here."

At some point that weekend, Ann tearfully confronted her husband and Pat Dillon, accusing the two of an affair. They denied it, and Scher refused to speak to her for the rest of the trip. Marty Dillon and Pat remained in stony silence as well.

It was the last time Ann ever saw Marty Dillon. She later regretted that she didn't take him up on that drink. She wonders now what he was thinking back then. Perhaps he would have told her.

After the Schers returned to Montrose, Ann asked her husband again if he was in love with Pat. This time, he gave a different answer. He said he was.

A month later, in September 1975, Stephen Scher told his wife that he had filed for divorce and that Marty Dillon was his lawyer. He told her the proceedings would be handled fairly and she didn't need her own attorney.

None of it, Ann later learned, was true.

At the time, she was thoroughly confused. She couldn't understand why Marty Dillon would agree to handle the divorce. She later decided it was an effective ploy to keep her from talking to Marty, from sharing her suspicions that their spouses were having an affair. In reality, it was Bob Dean, Marty's associate, who filed the divorce papers.

Even after he announced he was divorcing Ann,
Stephen Scher didn't leave the farm for two months,
until he was able to arrange to move into the Church
Street house. One night, Ann heard noises and asked
what he was doing. He told her he had a gun in the
bedroom, and he was pushing furniture against the
door because he was afraid of her. She learned later
that he'd told friends that he worried she might try to
kill him.

Ann wondered about that, years later. Was he trying to set her up? Look at the size of him versus her.
And if he was so afraid, she reasoned, why didn't he
just leave the house? Sometimes she thought he was
trying to make her feel as if she'd lost her mind. In
the last days of the marriage, she almost did.

Stephen Scher finally left the day before Thanksgiving. A distraught Ann asked him how she would
survive. At the time, she was working sixteen hours
a week at the New Milford clinic, making minimum
wage.

She never forgot his response. For months his
words echoed in her mind, at the lowest point of her
life. The man she'd married back in Milan, Michigan,
whom she'd helped put through medical school and
followed to New Mexico and then on to Pennsylvania, that day, as he left the farm, he told her she
wasn't worth anything, that she wasn't smart or pretty
enough to make anything of her life.

"I'm going to reduce you to living in a rented room
in Binghamton, working the night shift flipping ham-
burgers at McDonald's," he told her as he walked
out. As a final touch, Stephen Scher called the phone
company and had Ann's line disconnected.

He moved into the house at 85 Church Street. Now he and Pat had even more opportunities to be alone.

By the winter of 1976, just a few months before the death of Marty Dillon, the affair between Pat Dillon and Stephen Scher had become so blatant that numerous people witnessed them kissing and touching, seemingly oblivious to anyone else. Neighbors on Kelly Street picked up on the curious routine—Marty Dillon's BMW pulled out of the driveway every morning at eight-thirty; about twenty minutes later, Scher's gray Ford pulled in; a little before noon Scher would leave. At noon, Dillon's car would appear as he returned home for lunch. One neighbor, Judith Vaccaro, caught Pat and Steve Scher kissing in the driveway in the middle of the day. The teenage paperboy, Dan Calby, once knocked for several minutes before Pat Dillon hurried to the door, nervous and red-faced, her clothes askew, her hair mussed. Calby had seen Scher in the kitchen many times when he'd come to collect for the newspaper. This time the doctor was nowhere to be seen, yet his car was parked in the driveway.

At the hospital, nurses were astonished by how the couple behaved. Ann Bennett, a nurse's aide assigned to Pat, had never liked working for Pat and Dr. Scher—she told others she felt like a fifth wheel along on a date. One day in the winter of 1976, she had just finished cleaning the emergency room when she walked into what was known as the "drug room," where supplies were kept, to find Pat Dillon and Stephen Scher kissing. For a moment, Ann almost left, but then she decided, no she had a right to be there. Catching sight of her, Scher and Pat pulled away from each other, and everyone suddenly got busy.

Elaine Henninger worked at the switchboard and as a receptionist. She said nothing whenever Pat Dillon and Dr. Scher would go into room 13 just across from her desk, lock the door, and stay there for almost an hour.

Here we go again, she'd think. Henninger resented that it was left to her to appease waiting patients. What could she say to them? Now and then the young woman considered knocking on the door of room 13, but she never got up the nerve. She didn't even look up when Scher and Patty Dillon finally emerged; she felt too embarrassed. She wondered why they didn't.

In the spring of 1976, Sandra Jean Price, a registered nurse, saw Dr. Stephen Scher come up behind Pat Dillon, reach from behind, and squeeze her breasts. Pat turned, saw the doctor, and laughed. Sandra Jean Price did not. Around the same time, another nurse, Betty Williams, was filling an order for the clinic and walked into the drug room to find Pat Dillon on a stool reaching for something and Dr. Scher with his hands up her skirt. Dr. Scher saw her and pulled his hands away. On another occasion, Jocelyn Richards, a nurse's aide, witnessed almost exactly the same scenario.

Richards had worked at the hospital for many years and had known Dr. Scher since he first joined the staff. She always remembered a conversation they'd had in which they described their philosophies of life. She told him about her church and her connection to God. He told her he was an atheist. "If I want something, I get it one way or another," he said. "That's my philosophy of life."

In April 1976, Stephen Scher began to put the

pieces together in order to get what he wanted. He called a friend in New Mexico, Ken Jacobs, whom he'd met when he was a public health service officer almost a decade earlier. Scher liked the West, and he knew that the dry climate made it a good place for an allergy practice. He told Jacobs that he was going through a messy divorce and wanted to relocate. Scher wanted to know what he could expect in Las Cruces. He learned he would likely fare quite well.

It seemed like a perfect plan, leaving Montrose and starting anew. Only Dr. Stephen Scher did not intend to go alone.

Meanwhile, at 7 Kelly Street tension was high. In the last few months of his life, Marty Dillon retaliated against his wife's betrayal with long periods of silence. Pat, well aware of the reason, acted as if she couldn't understand why. "What did I do?" she'd ask her brooding husband. "Why don't you talk?"

For Marty Dillon, the humiliation had reached its peak—now even his parents knew what was going on. They were troubled by all the talk in town, all the rumors and innuendo about their daughter-in-law. Not long after Stephen Scher had moved out, Ann had cornered Marty's sister and told her that Steve was having an affair with Pat. Around the same time, a friend stopped Larry and Jo Dillon at the Montrose Inn and expressed condolences over the news that Marty and Pat were getting divorced. When the Dillons confronted their son and daughter-in-law, voices were raised and Pat Dillon ordered them out of the house. Marty later conceded that there were problems in his marriage but reassured his parents that things would work out.

His father wasn't convinced. Larry Dillon, recently

elected Montrose's mayor, was furious at his daughter-in-law for humiliating his son so publicly; he found her behavior shocking and disgraceful. He stopped into Marty's law office frequently and gave his son some advice. "You better get your house in order," he told him.

Then one night not long before Marty's death, Jo Dillon, on her way home from her daughter's house, saw the light on at 7 Kelly Street and dropped in. She found Pat and Steve sipping wine on the basement couch. Marty was upstairs sleeping.

Pat was furious at the intrusion. "I'll get him up for you, and you will no longer be welcome in this house," she told her mother-in-law.

Jo was heartbroken. When Marty emerged from the bedroom, his mother was practically shaking. "Is that true, Marty?" she asked, wiping away tears. "I won't be welcome in this house?"

Marty Dillon sighed. "Mom, the only one making sense here tonight is you."

By May 1976, Marty Dillon could no longer hide from the truth. A week after his thirtieth birthday, he changed his $50,000 life insurance policy, making his children beneficiaries instead of Pat. The marriage, he decided, was over.

He reached out to his friends. Over dinner with Anthony Amendola one night in May he confided that his marriage was in trouble. "Patty's seeing somebody else," he admitted. "It's Dr. Scher."

Another night, at the Montrose Inn, he confessed to his friend John Demmer the same suspicion.

But in the last weeks of his life, Marty Dillon must have had a change of heart. He told Kendall Strawn that he planned to give Pat an ultimatum—it was him or Dr. Scher. Kendall encouraged Marty, saying that it was about time.

When Marty finally gathered the strength to confront what he had refused to face for so long, the young attorney got the reaction he'd probably hoped for: Patty didn't want a divorce. She told him she would stay with him, that they would remain a family. Whether she admitted the affair or continued to deny it to Marty remains her secret.

But clearly she realized that things had to change, and she told Stephen Scher it was over. She would not be moving with him to New Mexico. Ironically, considering her affair, Patty used her religion as the primary reason. She told Scher she couldn't get a divorce, that she couldn't go against the tenets of Catholicism. She must have known, too, that Marty, an aggressive lawyer and a devoted father, would never let her leave Susquehanna County with Michael and Suzanne.

In truth, Patty Dillon wasn't prepared to take that final step. She couldn't face her family and all the people in town; besides, a part of her still loved Marty. Somehow, the affair had been different. She could ignore Marty for not being the adoring husband she'd wanted and at the same time savor the familiar childhood feelings of being the center of attention. But divorce pushed it all too far. She wouldn't do it.

Stephen Scher couldn't understand it. For him, the solution was simple: They'd just leave Montrose and everyone in it behind. He was not hearing what he wanted. He was not used to being told no. He tried to understand Patty's reluctance, but he could not.

And so just a few weeks before June 2, Stephen Scher went to visit Justine Jenner, a devout Catholic

who was a longtime patient of his. Jenner was aware
of his affair with Pat Dillon, and despite her religious
beliefs, she was nonjudgmental about it. She thought
the world of Dr. Scher. If he and Patty wanted to be
together, she thought they should be.

Scher told her he wanted to understand Catholicism. "If I could take Patty Dillon out of state, could
she practice her religion there?" he asked.

Jenner told him she could not. "The record goes
with you," she told him. "It's in her soul. She
couldn't go to confession and receive the sacraments
of our church. Your faith is inside you. You can't just
leave the state and practice faith in another state."

It was not the answer he was looking for. The doctor left, disturbed.

About that same time, Pat threw Marty a belated
surprise thirtieth birthday party. She asked Kerry Graham to spend the day with Marty at Gunsmoke and
keep him away from the house. Graham drove up
from his home outside Philadelphia, not far from
where Marty and Pat had lived as newlyweds while
Marty attended law school.

The two men shot about one hundred rounds and
then returned to the trailer. They opened beers and
sat talking on the porch. Alone with his closest friend,
Marty confessed his unhappiness. He never mentioned Stephen Scher, but choking back tears, he told
Kerry that he hadn't had sex with Patty for months,
that they were barely speaking, that his marriage was
coming apart.

Graham was surprised. He didn't live near the Dillons anymore, but he'd seen Marty and Pat on occasion and hadn't known there was trouble at home. He

could see his friend's anguish. He didn't know quite what to say.

It was almost eight when they finally returned to Kelly Street. As Marty walked downstairs into the recreation room filled with his family and friends to shouts of "Surprise!" his spirits were instantly lifted. He was delighted by the party, touched that his wife had made such an effort for him. Perhaps things were looking up for their marriage. Marty raised his glass and toasted his guests. About forty of them filled the room, smiling and holding up their glasses, too, in tribute to him.

Among them was Kendall Strawn. He was standing toward the back of the room, having purposely positioned himself so that he could see both Marty and Stephen Scher.

As Marty spoke to his friends, Strawn watched for Scher's reaction. The expression on the doctor's face as he stared at the young lawyer stunned Strawn—it was nothing short of hatred. It was a look Kendall Strawn would never forget, a gaze of such intensity, such loathing that it was almost a precursor of what was to come, a sign of the doctor's true feelings toward the man who stood in his way, who prevented him from getting what he wanted.

A short time later, when one by one his friends turned down an afternoon of skeet shooting and Marty energetically tried to find replacements, the young lawyer was clearly unnerved at the prospect of spending time alone with Dr. Scher. At the same time, Marty believed that the relationship between his wife and the doctor—whatever it had been—had ended. Patty's promise was enough.

And so going to Gunsmoke that day, while uncomfortable, was not unfathomable. Marty Dillon had submerged his feelings for so long that it was simply another example of the depth of his denial. He never suspected that peril awaited him in the woods.

But maybe on some level his wife did. She'd called his office that day, minutes after he'd already left, much to the surprise of Bonnie Mead. Marty's secretary knew that Pat almost never called her husband at work. That day, too, Mead picked up something different in Pat's voice—she sounded hurried and tense.

What thoughts swirled through her mind that afternoon? Did she suddenly feel a pang of uneasiness about her husband and lover alone in the woods? Did she wonder what words might pass between them, what the evening might bring?

Perhaps she sensed a denouement approaching and that realistically, only one man could win. And if there was to be only one victor, it would surely be the man who had the knowledge, the one who knew her dreams and desires, the man who had her loyalty. Tragically, it was a battle between unequals, for in his denial, Martin Dillon had relinquished his own power. In his trust of the two people who had so egregiously deceived him, he left himself vulnerable to a terrible evil he could not have imagined.

CHAPTER 5

It was just after seven when two borough police officers rang the doorbell at 27 Lincoln Avenue, interrupting a lively conversation between Larry and Jo
Dillon and their visitor, Sue Caterson, the couple's
closest friend. When Larry saw the officers he wasn't
alarmed. He was the town's mayor, after all, and it
wasn't unusual to find police at the door.

But within moments his world collapsed. He and
his wife gasped in anguish, holding each other, pray-
ing to God that what they were hearing was a terrible
mistake. Their son, the officers reported somberly,
had died in a shooting accident at Gunsmoke.

It was futile, he knew, but Larry Dillon asked if
the police were positive Marty was dead. One of the
officers radioed to the scene and swiftly received con-
firmation.

Jo Dillon reacted at once. "We must get to Pat,"
she said.

Larry and Jo Dillon immediately got in their car and headed to Kelly Street, followed by the Montrose police. When they arrived, they discovered Pat's father mowing the front lawn, and Pat, her mother, and the children were emerging from the house under construction next door.

Jo Dillon began to walk toward the group. She called out to Pat, her voice choked with emotion. "There's been an accident."

Pat instantly saw the agony on her in-laws' faces and the sober expression of the borough police. Her heart began to race. This was not supposed to happen.

"I'll spend the rest of my life taking care of Marty," Pat called out to no one in particular, her voice rising in fear.

A pledge, a promise. But it was too late. Was it guilt mixed with sorrow that washed through Pat as her mother-in-law shook her head?

"Marty's gone," Jo sobbed, unleashing a torrent of tears.

Over the next half hour, the phone rang nonstop, and neighbors gathered on the sidewalk, stunned by the news. With a heavy heart, Jo Dillon walked to Joann Reimel's house, to tell her of her brother's death. In the kitchen of 7 Kelly Street, Pat phoned Dr. Raymond Bennett at the hospital, who informed her that the body of her husband was still at the camp.

"They should do something," Larry Dillon said sharply when Pat got off the phone, "not leave him lying on the ground like an animal."

With that, Larry announced he was going to Gunsmoke. By then, Jo had returned and begged her husband not to go alone. She called her son-in-law, Alan Reimel, and asked him to drive.

By now, it was almost dark, and back at Gunsmoke Stephen Scher started to complain again of chest pain. He'd been at the scene with officials for more than an hour and was anxious to leave. The pressure was getting to him.

When he asked Susan Strope of the Silver Lake ambulance squad to drive him to Montrose General Hospital, Trooper Hairston did not object and neither did the coroner. Indeed, John Conarton thought it was a good idea. In his mind, the doctor's experience that evening had been extremely traumatic, losing his best friend the way he did. He might even be at risk for a heart attack from all the stress.

During the twenty-minute ride to Montrose, Susan Strope periodically observed her passenger, asking him how he was feeling. Each time, Scher said he was okay but then mentioned what he said was his greatest concern, what would now become of little Michael and Suzanne Dillon.

"I keep thinking about those little kids," he told Strope several times. "I'm going to have to take care of those children."

How nice that he cares so much for those poor fatherless children, Susan Strope thought.

At the hospital, Strope led Scher inside and left him with Dr. Bennett, then she headed back to Gunsmoke to pick up her husband. Despite his earlier claims of chest pains, Scher stayed only a few minutes at the hospital, just long enough to relate his account of the terrible accident once more and accept condolences from his colleague. He then walked home across Mill

Street, took a shower, and changed clothes. Shortly after he got home, Paul Kelly and his wife, Pam, knocked at the door. Kelly, a local attorney, had been a childhood friend of Marty's.

Upon seeing the couple, Scher immediately began to cry. He repeated his story again: the porcupine, the shotgun blast, how he'd tried to save Marty. The Kellys didn't question his sincerity—they didn't know him well and had not heard rumors of an affair between him and Pat. The couple gently offered their sympathies to the weeping doctor, and after a few minutes they left.

Word of the shooting death of Marty Dillon traveled quickly, and grief and shock permeated the small town. But the horror of the news was compounded for those who long suspected the affair between Scher and Pat Dillon and who believed the doctor capable of anything. For them, Scher's account of what happened at Gunsmoke was instantly dismissed as fiction.

Bonnie Mead was among them. After work, she'd gone to the Orange Roof in New Milford, an ice cream shop, and was told by the owner that Montrose police had been calling around town looking for her. The twenty-one-year-old secretary drove immediately to the police station.

When she arrived, grim-faced officers asked her the whereabouts of Marty's law partner, Robert Dean.

"He's out all evening," she told them. "Anything you want done, call Mr. Dillon."

They asked again. Once more, Bonnie told them that Dean was unavailable and they should call Dillon.

Then one of the officers placed his hand firmly on

her shoulder, his voice menacing. "Where is Bob Dean?" he demanded. "You have to tell us."

Mead told him that Dean was at an E. F. Hutton stock party at the Treadway hotel in Binghamton. When she asked why they needed to know, no one answered. She got in her car and headed home, baffled.

When Bonnie pulled into the driveway, her mother, Ruth Mead, met her on the front porch steps. From the look on her face, Bonnie instantly knew that something terrible had happened.

"Mom, what's going on?" she asked, her fear growing.

"You'd better come in and sit down," her mother said.

In the house, Ruth Mead broke the news. "This is terrible," she told her daughter softly. "Marty Dillon is dead."

Bonnie's reaction was lightning fast. "Oh my God," she cried. "Everyone canceled today at Gunsmoke. Steve killed him."

She put her head down on the kitchen table and wept.

Kendall Strawn echoed that sentiment. When Pat phoned him late that evening and told him there had been an accident at Gunsmoke and Marty was dead, Strawn listened silently, cursing his decision not to shoot skeet that day. He hung up the phone convinced that his friend had been murdered by Stephen Scher.

It wasn't only friends of Marty's who were suspicious. A trooper at Gunsmoke, unaware of any motive Scher might have had to kill Dillon, was circumspect as well. After the doctor left, Frank Zanin, the records and identification officer, pointed out numerous in-

consistencies with Scher's account of the victim falling on his gun. Zanin had investigated several
hundred death scenes, and this one didn't make sense.

"This couldn't have happened this way," he told
the coroner and the troopers at the scene, pointing to
Dillon's untied shoelace. "Look at his shoelaces, look
at the boot itself. It's tight coming up the leg. The
laces were just untied and laid this way. If he had
been running, the top of that boot and the rest of the
lacing would have been opened. It doesn't make
sense. Common sense tells you if you're running the
boot's going to open up. You can't run and not open
up that boot. It's impossible. And look at the cuffs of
the pants. If you're running, the pants are down—
there's no reason for them to be up."

Zanin noticed the unbroken clay birds under the
body's left arm by the wrist and the skeet-throwing
machine six feet away. Off from the right hand, about
three feet from the body, he saw a set of ear protectors
and sunglasses, spattered with blood. He could easily
make out the markings on Dillon's head where it had
been worn—it was the only area that wasn't spattered
with blood. Clearly, the victim had been wearing the
ear protectors, and someone had taken them off.

Zanin observed the position of the body, on its
back, arms outstretched, the hole dead center in the
chest. It was a large hole, not consistent with a contact
wound and not compatible with the story told by Dr.
Scher.

"It's too big to be a contact wound," the officer
told the others. "It's way over the size of the barrel
itself."

When Zanin questioned the blood on the left side
of the ground, Conarton explained that was caused by

the victim having been rolled over when he was found and given emergency treatment.

Zanin found that odd, too. The shot went right through the heart, he pointed out. There was no emergency treatment for that.

That's automatic, he thought. You can see from where it went in that it had to take out the heart. That's strange.

Frank Zanin continued to inspect the area. He saw the Ithaca double-barreled 20-gauge empty. Then he saw the Winchester in pieces.

"Which is which here?" he asked. "Who owns what gun?"

"Dr. Scher owns the gun," answered Conarton, motioning to the 16-gauge, "and that's the one that killed him."

Zanin's focus turned to the broken weapon. "What happened here?"

Conarton explained about Scher smashing the gun in anger as Zanin continued to inspect the firearm. The officer's doubts were growing. There was no blood on the gun, not on the inside or the outside of the barrel. With a contact wound, he knew, blood spatter blows back out, to the inside of the barrel and outside.

Zanin checked the distance. It was 252 feet from the trailer to the clearing. He measured the gun stand—98 feet from the trailer.

John Conarton was growing impatient. "This was an accidental shooting," he said. "A man was running with his shotgun. He tripped over his laces, the gun went off. It was an accident. Let's get some photos and that's it."

While Zanin took photos, Conarton went to the Dillon trailer to use the phone. He called Bartron's Funeral Home. The owner, Robert Bartron, was the deputy coroner. Conarton had worked with him for years.

"We're bringing you Martin Dillon from out at Gunsmoke," Conarton told Bartron. "There was a hunting accident."

Robert Bartron went downstairs to the preparation room to get ready. Although this was the kind of phone call he received every day, he felt particularly saddened this time. He and his wife were good friends of Larry and Jo Dillon. Barton had known Marty since he was a child.

At about eight-thirty the body of Martin Dillon was loaded into the Silver Lake ambulance at Gunsmoke, and Carol Gazda's husband Tom, and his partner, Kevin Bruster, drove out to Russin Road, headed for the funeral home in Montrose. Troopers John Salinkas and John Fekette, who only hours before had chatted with Marty on Public Avenue, followed the ambulance.

By now, Susan Strope had returned from taking Scher to the hospital, and she and her husband were on their way home when they recognized Larry Dillon and his son-in-law heading in to Gunsmoke. The Stropes knew the Dillons casually from ballroom dance clubs they all frequented. Don Strope also knew Larry and Jo from Montrose, where he'd grown up.

The Stropes pulled over and got out of their car, and Larry Dillon did as well. He walked over to them, his eyes suddenly very old. The look on his face brought back an anguished memory to Susan and Don Strope. Three years earlier, the couple lost their eighteen-year-old son, Donald Robert Jr., whom they called Bob. The young man had been scuba diving in nearby Silver Lake and had run out of air. When he tried to come to the surface, he rose too quickly and died of an embolism.

The Stropes felt overwhelming pity for the man who stood before them. They understood too well the pain that wracked through him.

"You know what this is like," Larry Dillon said softly, tears filling his eyes.

"We know," said Don Strope, reaching out his hand, "and we're so sorry."

There weren't any words to comfort Larry Dillon, the Stropes knew. Not at this moment, not ever. All they could offer were their prayers.

After the couple left, Larry Dillon and Alan Reimel proceeded to the scene. The coroner was still there, and so were some of the troopers. The two men went past the trailer and up the path. When Larry saw the pool of blood on the ground, he almost collapsed from grief. One of the troopers helped support the weeping man.

"Can't something be done about this?" Larry asked, almost in a whisper.

"Yes, Mr. Dillon," the trooper told him. "We'll take care of it."

For a while, Larry and Al Reimel stood sorrowfully by the spot where Marty had died. It didn't make sense to them. Marty tripped and fell in the exact spot where they'd been shooting the birds?

"Something's funny here," Alan Reimel told his father-in-law softly.

In the quiet of Gunsmoke, by the crest of the mountains and forests where Larry Dillon had taught his son to hunt so many years ago, the heartbroken man nodded. He thought so, too.

Most everyone had left by the time the two men decided to return to Montrose. Larry Dillon told Al Reimel to go on ahead—he would drive his son's BMW home. When Larry arrived back at 7 Kelly Street, Pat told him that Marty's body was at Bartron's Funeral Home and she wanted to see him. Larry did too.

Alan Reimel drove them and stayed in the car. When Larry and Pat were alone in the funeral home, waiting to be shown the body, Pat confronted her father-in-law. "Larry, you don't think Steve killed him, do you?" she asked.

Larry Dillon paused for a moment. "Pat, I don't know just what I think right now," he said quietly.

Pat Dillon just stared at him. "You bastard," she said sharply.

Marty Dillon's father and widow were ushered into the basement where his body lay, a large towel covering his chest. Larry couldn't bear to stay more than a few moments. Left alone, Pat lifted the towel, stared at the gaping hole in her husband's chest, and broke into tears.

Al Reimel drove Larry and Pat back to Kelly Street, and Larry went inside to get his wife. The Dillons were leaving when Stephen Scher's car pulled up. The three stood on the lawn for several minutes, as Scher haltingly explained what had happened to Marty and expressed his despair at losing his friend.

"I'm very upset," he told Larry Dillon. "I'm a very lonesome man."

Marty's father did not answer. He was in shock, in total disbelief that this was really happening, that his beloved son was gone and in front of him was Dr.

Stephen Scher, crying, talking about a terrible accident. As the Dillons drove away that night, spent, Stephen Scher headed inside 7 Kelly Street to see Pat.

It was another seminal moment in the doctor's life, when he faced the woman he loved and related his story about the death of her husband. If he was worried about her reaction, he needn't have been.

Pat was seated on the living room sofa clutching tissues. By now, a small crowd of friends and family had gathered. A neighbor was taking care of Michael and Suzanne.

Fighting back tears, Stephen Scher walked over to Pat and placed his hand gently on her shoulder. "I'm sorry this happened," he told her, his voice cracking. "He was chasing one of those damn porcupines, and he fell."

Standing in the living room that night, Dr. Stephen Scher once more recited the story he'd concocted, slightly different from the version he'd just told Trooper Hairston and John Conarton. This time he said that he and Marty had gone back to the trailer to get cigarettes and that they were inside when Marty spotted the porcupine. Dillon grabbed the nearest gun lying by the screen door and ran out. Then Scher heard the shot.

The thoughts running through Pat Dillon's mind as she heard her lover recount the death of her husband remain a mystery. Why would Marty, with his bad back, run with a loaded shotgun? He was so safety conscious; it didn't make sense. Why, too, would he have grabbed Scher's gun instead of his own? For that matter, why was he so intent on killing a porcupine?

If Pat Dillon suspected that Stephen Scher was lying, it wasn't apparent. Not on the evening of June 2 and not for the rest of her life.

It was to be the ultimate act of denial, the subconscious wish come true that somehow, miraculously, she could escape her marriage, change partners, and, most important, avoid the messy repercussions of divorce and the inescapable charges of her own infidelity. By accepting Stephen Scher's story, she could maintain the image she'd created in childhood of the good Catholic girl, the persona that mattered most to her. For just as Stephen Scher was now free to take over the life Marty Dillon had created, so, too, could Pat Dillon embrace a new role—the doctor's wife. It was a title that she had been taught meant something special. Earning it simply confirmed the message so definitive in her upbringing, that she was just a little bit better than everyone else.

But that night, as mourners filed in and out of 7 Kelly Street, emotion surged and Pat cried bitter tears, unleashing the pain of losing the man a part of her still loved, of guilt over her betrayal of him, and of fear for her and her children's future.

It was past midnight when the troopers and John Conarton finally left the funeral home. Alone in the basement, Robert Bartron started to embalm the body of Martin Thomas Dillon. Doubts about what he'd been told by Conarton troubled the deputy coroner. Like many others in the small town, Bartron had heard the rumors about Patty and Stephen Scher and often saw the two together, especially since his funeral home was across the street from the hospital. He didn't know what to think. He knew that many people in town disliked Scher, but Bartron never had any problem with him. The doctor had even delivered Bartron's son.

Later that morning, when Bartron noticed that an ecchymosis had formed on the body's left side—what looked like a large brown bruise—his concerns increased. The deputy coroner knew that any break in the circulatory system allowed the embalming fluids he'd injected as well as blood to spill into the surrounding tissue, forming the spot. But it was the position of the ecchymosis that disturbed him. How could a shot from a fall enter the body at that angle? It suggested to him that the shot had traveled right to left and downward rather than straight through his body. If Dillon had fallen, as John Conarton had told him, surely the path would have been upward.

Alone in the basement that morning, Robert Bartron's discomfort grew.

Of all the people who suspected that the death of Martin Dillon was not an accident, Ann Scher brought a particular knowledge. She not only knew about her estranged husband's love for Patty Dillon, she knew he was capable of killing.

Several years earlier she'd come home one night from showing one of the dogs to a Boy Scout group and found Shadow's kennel empty. The Schers had owned Shadow for a few years, and Stephen Scher himself had been training her for obedience. Lately, though, the dog hadn't been performing well. She kept failing recall—when Scher would beckon her, Shadow wouldn't budge.

Ann could tell that her husband was losing interest in the dog, and with his consent, she spoke to the breeder who had bought Shadow's mother to see if she was interested in buying Shadow. The breeder was.

The two women were in the process of negotiating a sale when Ann came home that evening and saw Shadow's run empty. She went into the house and found her husband watching television.

"Shadow's kennel is empty," Ann said. "Where is she?"

"I shot her," Scher said, his eyes never leaving the television.

It was dark, so Ann knew that he hadn't been working with the dog and grown frustrated or angry. He'd simply decided that Shadow no longer served a purpose. For Ann, all the marital problems seemed to pale against this new insight into her husband. He was a man she didn't know anymore. He frightened her.

And so when she learned about the death of Marty Dillon, Ann never doubted that Stephen Scher had once again arranged a situation to suit himself. At that point, though, Ann was almost too emotionally distraught to care.

Indeed, in an ironic twist, Ann Scher had tried to take her life the very day Marty Dillon was shot. In a further coincidence, her life was saved because a friend tried to reach her to tell her what had occurred at Gunsmoke.

For months after Stephen Scher moved out, Ann Scher had been contemplating suicide. The depression she'd been suffering as her marriage came apart grew deeper until at the end of May she'd had enough. She was exhausted emotionally and felt trapped and frightened. In the last year of her marriage, Ann had unwittingly signed over joint assets, bank accounts, Keoghs, and stocks to her husband. Scher had told her that it would be easier for them to buy stocks and securities if she presigned some papers. She later learned that he'd used her signature to take their assets out of her name.

He hadn't been able to take the real estate they'd bought together, but there was little equity as it was. Now, her checking account almost depleted, Ann had been putting in ten-hour days as a microbiologist at Binghamton General Hospital. Before work and late at night she cared for the dogs as well as feeding some thirty-five head of cattle and other animals. The responsibilities of the farm overwhelmed her. So did her loneliness.

She had decided she would take her life on the evening of June 2, when she had the next three days off from work. That way, no one would look for her.

Ann somehow managed to get through her shift from eight until six-thirty and then drove home, parking her car in a small shed where it would not be visible. She wrote a note to a friend, a nurse at Montrose General named Donna Sands, and carefully outlined what she wanted done with her animals and her possessions.

She didn't say why she wanted to die. Her self-esteem had ebbed so low that she didn't think anyone would care. In the most bizarre of coincidences, Ann Scher, knowing nothing of the events at Gunsmoke, took twelve Pertofranes, a handful of Triavil and several Percodan a few hours after her husband pulled the trigger of his 16-gauge Winchester.

At about nine-thirty she lay on the couch and hoped death would come quickly.

But life had more to offer Ann Elias Scher, and with the good fortune of a close friend's concern, her

suicide attempt failed. Earlier that evening Donna
Sands had phoned to tell Ann the news of the shooting at Gunsmoke and became worried when she
didn't get an answer. So Donna drove to the farm and
saw that Ann had parked her car in the shed, which
she knew was unusual. She tried the front door and
found it locked. Then she went to the rear of the
house and looked through the glass sliding door and
saw Ann's purse on the dining room table.

Her heart pounding, Donna Sands discovered an
open window and crawled through. She discovered
Ann stretched out on the sofa, barely coherent, her
pulse rapid. Sands quickly called an ambulance.

Ann Scher was admitted into the intensive care unit
of Montrose General Hospital just after ten o'clock
and treated for an overdose. The next morning, she
awoke to find Donna Sands and Dr. Jim Miller standing by her bed. Donna asked her if she was alert
enough to hear some news. Ann said she was.

Donna Sands told Ann Scher about the events of
the night before, that her estranged husband had been
skeet shooting with Marty Dillon at Gunsmoke, that
there had been an accident, and Marty Dillon was
dead.

Ann Scher just looked at them. For a moment, there
was silence. Then Ann spoke. "He killed him, didn't
he?"

CHAPTER 6

The day after her husband's death, Pat Dillon sat in the kitchen crying as various friends and family members came and went. Kathy Novitske was there, and so was Joyce Wilcox. Patty had drifted from them in recent years, but when the two women learned of the shooting, they hurried to her side. Neither had any idea of Pat's affair with Stephen Scher. At the kitchen table that day, they saw the same Patty they'd grown up with, now devastated by the loss of her husband.

Patty appeared almost numb with grief. She kept repeating that Steve had tried to save Marty's life, that he'd attempted cardiac massage and artificial respiration. She was too distraught to make funeral plans. Her mother, Laura Karveller, took over.

Pat's brother, Robby, helped out, too. He picked up the Dillons' baby-sitter, Cindy Klein, and brought her to the house to care for Michael and Suzanne. The children were puzzled by the turmoil at home. The evening before, their next-door neighbor, Nancy Frey, had taken them to the Orange Roof for ice cream and then tucked them into bed at her house for the night. But the unfamiliar surroundings proved too much for Suzanne. The little girl cried so much that around midnight Frey took her home to her mother. Frey was taken aback to find Stephen Scher seated in the living room. Living on Kelly Street, Nancy Frey couldn't help noticing how much time the doctor spent at the house when Marty wasn't home. Frey didn't know what to make of it, she just thought it seemed inappropriate that Scher was the one to comfort Patty the night her husband died.

Scher was there again the next day, in and out of the house. He put in an appearance at the hospital, talking quietly with Dr. Monroe Bertsch and Dr. Raymond Bennett about the accident and about his estranged wife's condition. At one point, he received an unsettling phone call from Susquehanna County detective Jock Collier. The intense yet soft-spoken fifty-eight-year-old lawman asked Scher to come to his office the following day and give a statement. The doctor said he would. He had little choice.

In the afternoon, a small group gathered in the basement of Bartron's Funeral Home to observe Dr. James Grace's autopsy of Martin Dillon. On hand were coroner John Conarton, Corporal Robert Uschowskas, Trooper Fekette, and Jock Collier. The doctor, a longtime family practitioner in town, was not a forensic pathologist.

Dr. Grace opened the chest and observed the wound, noting the size of the opening, 1¼ inches. He removed the plastic wad and pellets from the discharged shell and handed them to Trooper Fekette.

He didn't perform any tests, nor did he preserve any specimens or slides.

In the end, Dr. Grace prepared a simple, one-page report. He did not specify the manner of death, only the cause—a gunshot wound to the chest. It was up to the coroner to determine whether the death was an accident, suicide, or homicide.

Meanwhile, the Dillons, Pat, and the Karvellers met with Robert Bartron upstairs to plan the funeral. Calling hours would be held the next day, in the afternoon and evening, and the service, on Saturday morning, would take place at Holy Name of Mary where Pat and Marty had married eight years earlier. When Bartron asked whom Pat had selected to serve as pallbearers, she gave him several names, including Kerry Graham and Kendall Strawn. Then she spoke haltingly. "Steve has asked to be a pallbearer."

The Dillons did not say anything, nor did Robert Bartron. The funeral director silently wrote the name Stephen Scher on the list.

In the next morning's edition of the *Binghamton Press*, Montrose residents learned of the coroner's decision regarding the death of Martin Thomas Dillon.

> *The shooting death Wednesday night of Montrose lawyer Martin T. Dillon was ruled accidental yesterday by Susquehanna County Coroner John W. Conarton, of Great Bend.*
>
> *Conarton said the 30 year old victim ran out of his Silver Lake hunting cabin after hearing a noise in nearby woods. Dillon, son of Montrose Mayor Lawrence J. Dillon, apparently tripped and fell on the shotgun he was carrying. The*

*weapon discharged, striking the victim in the
chest, killing him instantly, Conarton said.*

*Dillon was accompanied on his hunting trip
by Montrose physician Dr. Stephen Scher. Conarton said the two were trapshooting.*

At eleven-thirty on June 4, 1976, Dr. Stephen Scher
gave a one-and-a-half-hour statement to Jock Collier.
Earlier Scher had stopped by Montrose General and
asked Gary Passmore and John Dabulewicz to accom-
pany him to the detective's office, and they agreed.
The two men sat outside District Attorney Ed Little's
office as Scher went into a small room with Collier
and a stenographer, Elaine Petrzala. Dr. Scher gave
his name, home address, telephone number, and social
security number.

Then Collier began to walk Scher through the
events of June 2, 1976.

"At this time I want you to relate to us what transpired earlier, as far as your getting together," he
said.

Scher took a deep breath and started to explain. He
told the detective how he, Gary, and sometimes Earle
Wootton usually got together to skeet-shoot a couple
of times a month, on Wednesdays. He explained that
Gary had canceled, and that he'd called Marty to see
if he still wanted to go. It was Marty, Scher said, who
insisted they go.

When three o'clock arrived and Marty hadn't
shown up, Scher said he figured Marty had gone to
borrow his father's Blazer to go to Gunsmoke. Then
at three-fifteen Marty pulled up in his BMW.

He told the detective how Marty wanted to drive
that day and how they switched the guns and am-

munition from Scher's car to the BMW. He explained
that they had several guns between them—a .38 special, two .22 pistols, a 20-gauge, a 12-gauge, and
Scher's 16-gauge. They drove up to Gunsmoke.

"We shot the birds, just like always," Stephen
Scher told Collier. "We were shooting doubles. Not
many, but we were trying. . . . We started with 10 a
piece and I would throw the bird then we would
switch."

They talked, Scher said, about the murder trial and
about Scher and Passmore's trip to visit a friend, Bill
Hancock.

"Everything was fine," he told Collier. "He said,
'Let's go shoot some more birds' so we went out and
took a couple more cans of beer, he took the clay bird
out and we went back shooting. We must have shot
another 18–20 rounds. . . . He asked if I had my cigarettes, I said no. He said, 'Let's go back to the cabin
and get some cigarettes.' . . . We went back to get a
cigarette, we walked down the path where the shooting bench is just about that far when he stopped. He
heard a rustling and he said, 'Did you see it?' I said
no. He moved down toward the bench. I followed
where he was pointing, to the right of the cabin. There
was something out there, the brush moving, something gray. I don't know what it was. I didn't see
when he saw it. He thought it was a porcupine. He
said, 'Wait right here,' his last words. He was running
up the path. I just watched him. He knew I had the
things in the tube . . . I heard the click then a shot.
Then I yelled, 'What the hell are you shooting for
way back there, you turkey, you can't even see it.' I
called, no answer. I knew something was wrong when

he didn't answer the second time. I walked up the path and he was lying there.''

Jock Collier listened intently. ''How did you observe Marty?'' he asked.

''I put my hand into the hole thinking if he nicked the aorta or something along that line the idea would be to stop the bleeding,'' Scher said. ''I took my hand out momentarily and then I started mouth to mouth. There was no beating.''

''You found him on his front?''

''By his side or belly and I had to turn him over. I tried doing these things, it was hopeless.''

''Do you know where the gun was?''

''No. I couldn't believe what happened. I stood up, I walked around.''

''After you tried to help him?''

''Yes. Then I figured I better go call somebody. I ran down the path, past the cabin toward the road. I started getting chest pains.''

Scher went on to recount how he took the car keys out of Dillon's pocket and drove to Andrew Russin's house. He told Collier that when he returned with Russin he noticed the gun in front of Marty's head, at the base of the tree.

Collier asked him if he hadn't noticed it before, after he'd tried to resuscitate Marty.

''All I saw was my best friend lying on the ground,'' Scher responded.

''How was he lying, was he stretched out, hunched up?''

''No, he was hunched up. He was on his side, partly on his belly. His legs were not hunched up.''

''You said the gun was pointed away from his head?''

Scher explained that the barrel was pointing toward Marty's head, no more than three feet away. He told Collier he had planned to give Marty the gun as a gift.

"Do you recall when you were done shooting and what Marty did with his gun?" Collier asked.

"I imagine it was either against the tree or lying on one of the stumps. We shot each other's guns."

"That day?"

"Yes, everyday he was doing much better than I was. He was even trying doubles with my pump."

"You said you were going back for cigarettes, did you run out?"

"No, we didn't have any there. We apparently left them in the cabin."

"You were going to quit when you went back to the cabin?"

Dr. Scher began to get agitated. Collier kept firing questions. It seemed to Scher that the detective wasn't buying his story.

"I have a feeling you don't understand anything I said," Scher said brusquely.

Jock Collier decided to move to another topic. He asked Scher what his marital status was, and the doctor told him he was getting a divorce and that Marty had been handling it.

Collier asked about Ann's condition, and Scher said he didn't know.

"I can't tell you now," he said. "She is in the hospital. She apparently tried to overdose herself. I went to talk to her, she doesn't want to talk to me. . . . I talked to her sister and she has been threatening this. I talked to friends of hers, Sands and other people. She raises dogs and one died and she has gone downhill since.''

At that point, Jock Collier asked Stephen Scher to collect the clothing he wore that night, and the doctor agreed to turn it over. Then the detective questioned him about the ear protectors and sunglasses Marty had on.

''They were on his shoulder,'' explained Scher, ''but as he went running up I am sure he went to put them on. I don't know if he had his glasses on. I remember moving them when I flipped him over. I took the ear protectors off his head when I started the mouth to mouth. I flipped him over, the blood was gushing out. I put my hand in the hole to find the aorta. There was no beat.''

It was almost one o'clock. Jock Collier didn't realize it then, but his interview with the doctor would end with his next question.

''You never had any disagreement?'' he asked.

Stephen Scher said no. ''We were discussing about this rumor,'' he told the detective. ''I told him I was thinking of leaving town. It was rough on him. He sat and told me I was just a quitter and chicken, 'Don't run away. It was just small people talking.' ''

There was silence in the small conference room. Stephen Scher suddenly got up and walked over to the window. He stared outside, tense. Jock Collier waited. The detective knew he'd struck a nerve.

But Scher was finished talking. He told Collier that he'd had enough, that he was leaving. Before the detective could say anything, Scher walked out. He would never again speak to the detective—or to anyone else in law enforcement.

That afternoon, Scher, in dark glasses, showed up

at Bartron's Funeral Home for the wake and never left Pat's side. Later, when family and close friends gathered at 7 Kelly Street, Scher continued to recount the events of the previous day. Kerry Graham was particularly interested in hearing Scher's story. He'd learned of his best friend's death when he happened to phone the Dillon home around eight the very night of the shooting, asking for Marty. Graham had been thinking about his friend since their conversation at Gunsmoke a couple of weeks earlier, when Marty had forlornly confessed his unhappiness over his marriage. Graham figured he'd check in and see how he was doing.

Pat had picked up the receiver and told him that Marty was dead, there had been an accident. Now, standing in the Dillons' living room with Dr. Stephen Scher, Kerry Graham had an overwhelming sense that his friend had been murdered.

That evening, at the Montrose Inn, where Marty had gone for lunch or cocktails after work almost daily, the usual crowd of young people packed the bar. Robert Bartron stopped in and surveyed the scene with nothing short of amazement. Although there were close to one hundred people surrounding the bar, there was virtual silence in the room.

I guess that age group wanted to be together today, Bartron thought. He stayed a short time and then left. The sadness in the room was too unsettling.

Hundreds filled the pews at Holy Name of Mary the next morning for Martin Dillon's funeral. The sadness of the morning reached its peak at the cemetery, when mourners dropped flowers onto the casket.

Among the grievers that day was detective Jock Collier. He watched stonily as Dr. Stephen Scher, clad in a dark suit, his eyes cast down, helped carry Dillon's casket. Later that day, the detective called the doctor, wanting to meet again. Collier wasn't the least bit satisfied with what he'd heard the day before. He had many additional questions.

But Stephen Scher was taking no chances. He didn't return the detective's call and discussed the situation with Pat. It was she who told him to consult with Peter O'Malley, a Waverly criminal defense attorney whom Marty had respected. Scher immediately called the attorney at home and went to see him later that day.

Sitting on the front porch of his home, joined by two of his partners, O'Malley told Scher to recount the events of June 2 slowly, with as much detail as possible.

Stephen Scher explained about returning to the trailer for cigarettes and how Marty had seen a porcupine, grabbed his gun, and run off. He told O'Malley about hearing the gun click and the shot, and how he couldn't see what had happened from where he stood. He said he'd tried to resuscitate his friend, that he'd attempted cardiac massage. He confessed how he'd broken the gun in frustration and how he'd wept for Marty's two little children.

When Scher finished, O'Malley left him on the porch and went into the house with his partners. The three concurred that the doctor's story was sound. They even agreed that they would permit Scher to take a polygraph test, under controlled circumstances. Then O'Malley announced that he would return Jock Collier's phone call.

"We have nothing to hide," he told his partners.

At the end of their three-hour consultation, O'Malley told Stephen Scher that he had nothing to worry about. Scher left, much relieved.

But when O'Malley got Collier on the phone and identified himself as Stephen Scher's attorney, the attorney quickly realized he'd been too optimistic.

An angry Jock Collier made no attempt to conceal his disgust toward Stephen Scher. "That bastard. He killed Larry Dillon's kid."

Peter O'Malley reacted just as swiftly. "You've already made up your mind," he said curtly. "You've just closed the door."

Collier was furious. "You don't give us cooperation, we're going to arrest him."

The attorney was nonchalant. He loved a good fight. "That's your option. But check with the DA's office to see whether you're covered under the liability counsel, because if you don't have a case, we're coming after you for malicious prosecution."

When Scher told Pat what had transpired between O'Malley and Collier, she decided to call Jo Dillon and ask her to come up to Kelly Street. She wanted to discuss what Larry Dillon was doing.

"I want to talk to you because you're the stronger of the two," Pat explained tersely.

She told Jo Dillon that Steve felt badly about the accident and was fearful that he was going to be arrested. Pat complained that Larry was stirring up trouble. She asked Jo to convince her husband to stop inciting authorities to investigate.

"Larry is pushing this," Pat said angrily. "It's all political. The DA wants to make a name for himself."

Pat was mistaken. District Attorney Ed Little was

not behind the initial inquiry in the days after Marty Dillon's death. It was Jock Collier. And the detective didn't need encouragement from Larry Dillon—he firmly believed there were inconsistencies with Scher's story and a multitude of unanswered questions.

On Monday, less than a week after the shooting, Collier and troopers Fekette and Salinkas went to Montrose General Hospital and met briefly with Scher. They asked the doctor to take a polygraph, and Scher replied that on advice from his lawyer he would not. The men did manage, however, to retrieve the clothes Scher wore that day, pulling them out of the hamper in the doctor's bathroom.

Then Jock Collier called Scher's attorney, Peter O'Malley. "Are you going to bring him in?" he asked.

"I made my position clear," O'Malley said. "No statement, no lie detector test, based on the conversation we had."

In his cramped office on Public Avenue, across the street from where Marty Dillon had practiced law, Jock Collier typed a one-page letter to District Attorney Ed Little. He explained that although John Conarton had issued a tentative verdict of accidental death, the coroner agreed to change his verdict if an investigation warranted it. Collier was certain that it did.

The detective maintained that the possibilities of the death as suicide or by accident were not plausible. He strongly urged Little to press the Pennsylvania state police for a thorough examination of the case:

From personal knowledge of Subject, his Religion, his care-free state of mind at 1530 hours

*when he talked to Troopers Fekette and Salin-
kas in Montrose, Rule out any possibility of de-
liberate self destruction. An examination of the
scene, angle of the wound of entrance, and information available at present are not satisfac-
tory to this investigator as being caused by a
fall on the weapon. The physiognomy of one
subject, his partial destruction of Weapon, and
his explanation of the incident are not satisfac-
tory to this Investigator.*

Jock Collier ended with a warning. "Time is vital
at this point. We must have all photographs for intensive examination, Laboratory reports, and further interview with persons who may have any knowledge,
as well as re-interviewing subjects with information
of importance."

To Collier's enormous disappointment, Ed Little
refused to heed his advice. Like John Conarton, the
district attorney simply did not believe that a respected doctor gunned down a well-known attorney
in the peaceful hills of the Endless Mountains—even
though Little himself was representing Ann Scher in
her divorce and knew of the charges of an affair between the doctor and his nurse, even though Little
respected Jock Collier and ordinarily considered his
assessment of a case beyond reproach.

It was to be the great tragedy in the town of Montrose. Contrary to Pat Dillon's claim that Ed Little
would prosecute Stephen Scher to make a name for
himself, it seemed to the locals that the small-town
district attorney was simply intimidated by Dr. Stephen Scher, a man who would undoubtedly hire the
best lawyers and vigorously fight any charges against

him. For Little it may have appeared to be a case he couldn't win.

And so with the DA unwilling to press for an inquiry, the troopers' commanders uninterested in pursuing the case further, and the coroner convinced that his initial ruling of accidental death was correct, the rumors and talk in Montrose remained exactly that. Left to issue his own conclusion, John Conarton signed the Local Registrar's Certification of Death for Martin Thomas Dillon on June 12, 1976, and checked "accident." Next to the question, "How did injury occur?" the coroner simply wrote what Dr. Stephen Scher had tearfully told him ten days earlier, as dusk settled at Gunsmoke.

"Running with gun," he penned. "Fell, gun went off."

CHAPTER 7

Within six weeks of Marty's death, Pat Dillon took her children and moved to an apartment in Gladwynne, just outside of Philadelphia, about a three-hour drive from Montrose. She got a job giving childbirth classes at Lankeau Hospital and arranged for preschool for Michael and Suzanne. She rented the Kelly Street house to an elderly couple and told the realtor to put the house up for sale when the one-year lease ended. The young widow had no intention of returning to Montrose.

She sold her husband's red BMW and phoned Kendall Strawn to tell him that he should keep the race car that he and Marty had bought together. She told him Marty would have wanted him to have it.

Pat would discover she would receive nothing from Marty's $50,000 life insurance policy, that he'd switched his beneficiaries to the children. As fate would have it, confirmation of the change arrived in the mail on June 2, the day Marty died. Once his death was ruled an accident, the money was placed in trust for Michael and Suzanne until they turned twenty-one.

For a while, Pat stayed in touch with a few of her childhood friends, including Kathy. In letters and phone calls she explained that she was sad to leave Montrose, but she couldn't stay; the rumors were flying, and she didn't want her children to hear the gossip. She told people that the thought that Scher had anything to do with her husband's death was too ridiculous even to consider.

To Pat, Dr. Stephen Scher was a healer.

He was also a man closing in on his goal. In the months following that day at Gunsmoke, he drove to Gladwynne on weekends to see Pat and the kids, toting bags filled with groceries and new clothing and toys for Michael and Suzanne. He'd play with the children, help get them ready for bed, kiss them goodnight. Late at night, he and Pat talked for hours. With masterful aplomb, Stephen Scher empathized with Pat over the guilt she carried about their affair and shared her sorrow over Marty's tragic accident.

Pat Dillon trusted him and believed what she wanted to believe. When some of her friends casually questioned Scher's frequent visits, Pat shot back that she was alone with two small children and he was the only one willing to help her. In private, she may have rationalized that Marty hadn't been there for her, had pushed her aside, didn't appreciate or love her, not the way Scher did. She had been lonely in her marriage. And so had Stephen Scher. They came together out of need.

Over Thanksgiving weekend, just five months after

Marty's death, she went shopping with Dr. Stephen Scher at a Wanamakers department store in Philadelphia. As they strolled through the lingerie department and Pat held up a cream-colored satin nightgown, Scher, his arm draped around her shoulder, nodded in approval.

A few yards away, Myron Ripis watched in amazement. He and his wife lived in Montrose and had known Pat, Marty, and Stephen Scher from the Montrose Inn. Ripis had even been to Scher as a patient once or twice.

Ripis and his wife had been visiting their son in college and stopped at the store to pick up some items. Ripis did not approach Scher and Pat, but he discussed what he'd seen with his wife, who shared his disapproval. The Ripises were aware of the talk around Montrose. This just seemed to confirm the rumors.

By this time Stephen Scher was shoring up his own arrangements to leave Montrose. He'd already negotiated an early end to his contract with the Medical Arts Clinic at Montrose General and flown to Las Cruces, New Mexico, in early November to rent an office and hire a nurse and secretary. He drove several hours north to Santa Fe and passed the oral exams for his New Mexico medical license.

A few weeks later, his divorce from Ann was final. In the bill of particulars submitted by Bob Dean, Marty's former partner, Scher accused Ann of paying more attention to her dogs than to him, refusing to have sex with him, and keeping an untidy home. He claimed that the trouble in the marriage began in the late part of 1968. "Defendant has offered such indignities to his person as to render his condition intolerable and life burdensome, a course of conduct which evinced an utter want of affection and sympathy for him and which was continually characterized with hatred, settled malice, disrespect, ill treatment, unkindness, neglect, abuse and malicious insults, also humiliating, mortifying, embarrassing and degrading.''

The most astonishing charge came at the end. With amazing hubris Stephen Scher lashed out at his estranged wife for accusing him of cheating on her with Patty Dillon. ''For several years Plaintiff and Defendant were friends of Attorney Martin Dillon and his wife, Patricia Dillon, and in 1975 the four of them went on a combined business trip and vacation, during which the defendant made vicious and hysterical remarks in front of the Dillons, insinuating and accusing the plaintiff of an affair with Patricia Dillon, all of which was unfounded and was so embarrassing to the Dillons and the Plaintiff that they cut their vacation short and returned to Montrose. . . . After the incident mentioned in paragraph 10 the defendant talked to various people in and around Montrose, making unfounded and false accusations accusing plaintiff of an illicit affair with Mrs. Dillon and accusing him of being the father of one of the Dillon children. All of which was extremely embarrassing to Plaintiff.''

But Scher's indictment of his wife didn't fool everyone. Judge Donald O'Malley at the Susquehanna County Courthouse lived just across Kelly Street from the Dillon house, and he, too, had seen Stephen Scher's car parked in the driveway every morning after Marty had left for work. When the Scher divorce came to his chambers, O'Malley, unwilling to compromise his own opinion, recused himself from hearing it.

On Christmas Day, Pat took Michael and Suzanne to Montrose and spent the evening at Larry and Jo Dillon's. The couple greatly appreciated her gesture. The first holidays without Marty were devastating, and being with his children helped enormously.

The Dillons knew that Pat had been spending time with Stephen Scher. Word traveled about the shopping trip at Wanamakers, and others, including Joyce Wilcox and Kerry Graham, had seen the two together in Gladwynne as well.

Larry Dillon, convinced that Stephen Scher had killed his son, was chilly toward Pat, but Jo Dillon went out of her way to be kind to her former daughter-in-law. Marty's mother agonized over what she and her husband reasoned had likely happened in the woods—that Scher and Marty argued, and Scher shot him. Jo wondered at times if perhaps they were wrong, if Marty wouldn't approve of their conclusion, if they were being unfair to Stephen Scher. She wrote to one of Marty's friends about it. "I wonder if Marty's saying, 'Knock it off, Mom and Dad, it was an accident.' Or if he's saying, 'It was not an accident. Don't let Pat trust Steve. He isn't our friend. He must not raise Mike and Suzy.'"

On another occasion Jo told Pat that she didn't know whether to feel sorry for Steve or hate him; Pat replied that Jo's words were degrading to Marty's memory.

And so Jo Dillon placed her faith in God and prayed that nothing would come of Pat's relationship with the doctor. She reminded herself that it was really not her business. At the same time it was excruciating to think that the man who might have caused her son's death could become her grandchildren's stepfather. She hoped that Pat would find someone else to share her life, to help raise Michael and Suzanne as Marty would have wanted.

It wouldn't happen. Stephen Scher and Pat Dillon stayed in constant contact after he left Montrose for good in early January, a few days after he performed a tonsillectomy on little Michael Dillon. In Las Cruces, Scher moved into an apartment complex, opened his office, and within a short time built a flourishing practice. He and Pat talked daily on the telephone.

The following May, Scher suffered his second heart attack, and Pat flew to his side. A few weeks later, Scher returned to the East Coast to see a cardiologist at the University of Pennsylvania hospital and stayed with Pat and the children for almost a month.

The first anniversary of Marty Dillon's death passed quietly. Three months later, in September 1977, Pat accepted an offer for the Kelly Street house from Willard and Linda Lewis, a young couple with two small daughters. Willard was a fifth-grade social studies teacher at Montrose Elementary School; Linda was an operating room nurse whom Pat knew from the hospital. After a brief negotiation, they agreed to a price: $46,500. Pat was delighted. She'd been anxious to sell, and she told the Lewises she was glad someone she knew was getting the place.

A few months later, Scher flew to Philadelphia and took Pat to a bat mitzvah for his cousin's daughter in New Jersey. The following April, Pat returned to Las Cruces for a few days.

It was during this visit that the couple decided to

get married. By now, almost two years had passed since Marty's death. It seemed to both of them that they had waited long enough.

But first, Stephen Scher made a phone call—to Peter O'Malley.

The lawyer didn't recognize Scher's name when his secretary gave him the message. "Put him on hold," O'Malley told her. "See if you can find a file."

When his secretary handed him a folder and he saw the Dillon name, it came back to him. Peter O'Malley picked up the receiver, upbeat. "Hello, Doctor, how are you? *Where* are you?"

"I'm out practicing in Las Cruces, New Mexico," Scher told him. "It's good country for allergy, and I like the climate."

They chatted for a few minutes. Then Peter O'Malley got to the point. "What can I do for you?"

"Pat and I are thinking of getting married," Dr. Scher said plainly.

O'Malley blanked again. "Pat?" he asked.

"Marty's widow," Scher replied. "We wonder if it would be all right."

Now Peter O'Malley understood. He laughed. "Doctor, I'm a lawyer, not a minister. Why are you calling me?"

Dr. Scher explained. "After this thing happened there was some rumbling in the community. Marty's father was saying I did it, that somebody's going to pay for it. You know how those communities are. I wonder if I married her if it would cause a lot of problems."

"Well," O'Malley said, "I can't tell you whether it would or wouldn't. But if they had a case against you they would have done something in the last two years. I don't think anyone's going to give you a rough time. Have a happy life together. Put Pat on the phone so I can congratulate her.''

Two months later, on June 18, 1978, Stephen Scher and Pat Dillon were married in Las Cruces in a simple ceremony attended by Michael, seven, and Suzanne, five. For the Dillon children, memories of their father by now had all but faded.

Larry and Jo Dillon learned of their former daughter-in-law's marriage to Dr. Stephen Scher by chance. The day after the wedding, Jo called Pat's number in Gladwynne, and an unfamiliar voice answered. The landlord told her that Pat and the children had moved.

Jo phoned her daughter and asked her to call Pat's mother. But when Joann Reimel reached Laura Karveller, Pat's mother was evasive, refusing to reveal Pat's whereabouts. She told Joann that the Dillons would receive a letter in the mail from Pat.

Two days later, they did. By then, Larry and Jo had already heard from others in town that Pat was in New Mexico, married to Stephen Scher. They read the letter from Pat with a heavy heart.

> Dear Jo & Larry,
>
> I feel that I should be the one to tell you that the children and I have moved to New Mexico, and that Steve and I are married.
>
> I am fully aware of your feelings for me as well as your hostility for Steve and have been advised that a face-to-face confrontation would be pointless. I will never be able to change your thinking, and will no longer try to do so.

It is not difficult to imagine your anger. I can only hope that when your fury subsides, you will choose to continue to be the children's grandparents. You will be welcome in our home at any time you wish to visit the children, and I will encourage any kind of relationship that you choose to have with them.

Pat

Two days later, Jo Dillon responded.

Dear Pat,

After two sleepless nights, your letter arrived in Wednesday's mail. We were not angry—I guess the word is hurt that half the town knew before us that you had moved; and not furious— just disappointed that you didn't feel you could tell us your plans and give us the opportunity to say goodbye to the children before they went so far away. I am sure good, well-meaning friends advised you to handle the situation the way you did, but they are friends that do not know the heart of Jo Dillon, and I guess you don't either if you feel my feelings toward you are unkind. I am sorry there is this misunderstanding in our personal relationship. However, time may heal this too.

We appreciate the fact that you will allow us to remain in contact with Mike and Suzie. My life would be empty without their love and the love of Paul and Jeff. Thank you for the invitation to visit them in your home. I hope in turn you will allow them to visit us, their grandparents.

*Larry and your father had a good visit after
your letter arrived. I hope you will keep in touch
with us about the development of the children.
Whatever your feelings toward us, I am certain
you know what Mike and Suzie mean to us.*

   Love,
   Jo

In her next letter to her former mother-in-law, Pat
softened, apologizing for the way she'd handled the
move, stressing that she hadn't meant to hurt them.
She sent pictures of the children in their swimsuits,
splashing in a pool. She reiterated that she would
never take Marty's children from them, but she
needed to move on with her life.

*Believe it or not, the decision to leave as I did
was an agonizing one. I know how you love the
children and at least as a woman and mother I
have always felt a bond with you. I would have
loved to discuss all of this with you, but unfor-
tunately you could not be my only consideration.*

   *If nothing else, I want you to know that I love
Marty's and my children more than anything in
this world and that my love for him will forever
live in the children.*

   *I will never minimize your loss, but neither
will you ever know the suffering we've all endured. I never want Mike and Suzy to hurt
again, and I'll do everything I can to see to it
that they enjoy a happy, healthy childhood.
Surely on this we all agree.*

   They are happy and enjoying their new home.

As you can see from the pictures, they are taking swimming lessons and are becoming little fish.

Whatever the situation between us, I am deeply grateful that you have chosen to remain close to them. They love you and I truly want them to know and love and be close to their grandparents. I promise to foster that relationship as much as possible.

We will send more pictures soon.

Love,

Pat

CHAPTER 8

For a few years after his son's death, Larry Dillon stopped into the office of Marty's former partner, Bob Dean, practically every week, begging Dean to encourage the Pennsylvania state police to investigate the shooting. Dean, a revered attorney in Susquehanna County, was active in local politics. His support could make a difference.

But Bob Dean was adamant. Not only was he convinced that Dr. Scher was incapable of murder, Dean had yet another theory on how Marty Dillon died—he thought the young man had killed himself. With all the talk of marital strife and with Marty changing his life insurance, it made sense to Bob Dean. The attorney had an answer for the argument that Marty couldn't have reached the trigger—he decided his former officemate rigged the gun somehow. Dean also maintained that John Conarton had done the family a favor by ruling the death accidental so that Michael and Suzanne could collect the insurance money.

Larry Dillon never swayed from his certainty that something else had happened at Gunsmoke. From the start, he found staunch allies in Jock Collier and Bonnie Mead. The detective and the secretary felt as strongly as he did that Stephen Scher had killed Marty. Jock, especially, battled enormous frustration in not being able to convince the DA and the state police to examine the case. It exasperated the detective that it wasn't within his jurisdiction to investigate further. Indeed, the Pennsylvania state police made it clear: The death had been ruled accidental; there was nothing to discuss.

Throughout the summer following Marty's death, Scher had kept a low profile in town, trying to steer clear of Collier. The detective continued to call him, repeatedly asking him to return for further questioning. For a few weeks, Scher stalled, making tentative appointments, then canceling. Then, on advice of his lawyer, he said he would not speak anymore about that day at Gunsmoke.

Jock kept the pressure on. Every month, just to unnerve the doctor, he'd show up at the clinic and request Scher take his blood pressure. On more than one occasion, when the two passed each other in town, the detective called the doctor a murderer.

Jock was disturbed when Scher moved to New Mexico, and he phoned the local and state police in Las Cruces to let them know that the doctor was suspected of a homicide. Later, when Collier learned that Scher and Pat Dillon had married, he wasn't at all surprised.

Several times a year, Jock and Larry met for hours

in Jock's cramped office, discussing the facts gathered from the scene, reviewing Scher's statement, searching for a way to bring attention to the discrepancies. Chain smoking Camels, Jock Collier promised Larry Dillon that one day he'd get the case looked at.

He told Bonnie Mead the same thing. Most mornings he'd see the young secretary when he picked up his coffee and doughnuts at the shop next to Bob Dean's office.

"Bonnie, I'm fighting an army," Collier often told her quietly.

Jock was born Willard Collier in the town of Oakland in the northwest tip of Susquehanna County, about twenty-five miles from Montrose. He grew up extremely poor and attended school only through eighth grade. In 1942, just before he was sent to the Pacific to serve in the military police in World War II, he married Alice Fisher, the mother of an eight-year-old boy, Kenny. When he returned in 1945, the threesome moved to the town of Susquehanna, a few miles west of Oakland.

Tall and muscular, his hair prematurely graying, Jock began working in a junkyard, pressing and loading scrap metal, but within a few months the Susquehanna chief of police position came open, and Collier got the job. The town board paid him just $5,600 a year, the same salary he'd receive for the next two decades. But money never mattered to Jock—all he'd ever wanted was to be in law enforcement.

For twenty-five years the taciturn Jock Collier kept the peace in the hardscrabble railroad town. He hauled drunks out of the Susquehanna movie theater, wordlessly lifting them by the seat of their pants with one hand. He apprehended thieves and wife beaters alone, with no backup. On several occasions he ran gangs of gun-toting gamblers out of the county. At home or behind the wheel of his car, he'd squeeze a rubber ball for hours, strengthening his hands.

At the same time, Jock had a gentle side and was beloved by the community. He'd give kids' rides in his police car, collect food and toys for poor families at Christmas, and help those he'd sent to jail put their lives together after they were released.

Jock Collier was an ambitious man. He read voraciously, studying history, wars, and anything related to law enforcement. He befriended doctors and learned about medicine. He knew as much about law as most attorneys. In the 1950s he became interested in photography and started taking pictures of crime scenes, developing them in a closet at home. At one time, he took an FBI correspondence course and scored so highly he was invited to attend the academy. He badly wanted to go, but the county couldn't afford to pay his salary while he was away, and by then, he and Alice had a son, Glenn. With a wife and two children to support, Jock turned down the offer. As it was, the family barely scraped by on Jock's pay. Most weekends he'd take his stepson Kenny and collect scrap metal to earn extra cash.

In 1960, he took a part-time job as Susquehanna County detective, based out of Montrose. It was in town a decade later that Jock Collier first met Marty Dillon, fresh out of law school and working for Bob Dean.

So impressed was Collier that he occasionally mentioned the young attorney to Kenny and his wife, Erika. The couple remembered the name. It wasn't often that Jock spoke so highly of someone.

"This kid is sharp," he told them. "He's not just a regular attorney. He's going to make it big."

After Dillon's death, Jock discussed his doubts about the accident with his stepson. He talked about the doctor's gun, the high brass shot, the angle and size of the wound, and all the inconsistencies in Scher's statement to Trooper Hairston and to him.

"Too many things don't match up," Jock told Kenny. "I know he did it."

Ken Fisher couldn't recall his stepfather ever being wrong. He knew that unless Jock was certain, he wouldn't say anything. And Jock, he knew, was a master at reading people.

Less than a year after Marty's death, Jock's assistant chief of police, Dick Pelicci, was elected Susquehanna County Sheriff, and Jock resigned as chief of police and took over the county detective position full time. Kenny took Jock's old job as Susquehanna Chief of Police.

Now that he was in Montrose even more, Jock brooded over the Dillon case. Around the holidays, especially, Jock became melancholy, talking even less than he normally did. Often he'd stop by the Fishers' house and sit silently at the kitchen table for hours, watching his grandchildren play.

His daughter-in-law, Erika, would bring him coffee and try to get him to open up. Sometimes after a week or so of daily visits, barely speaking a few words, he'd mention Marty Dillon, or Stephen Scher, and suddenly the Fishers understood.

Oh, God, *that's* what's the matter, Erika Fisher would think.

He reacted the same way in the days following his meetings with Larry Dillon. Yet in his heart, Jock

Collier trusted that the day would come when Stephen Scher would be prosecuted for murder. And just in case the doctor thought he'd been forgotten, the detective kept in touch.

Every December, Jock Collier bought a simple Christmas card and addressed the envelope to Dr. Stephen Scher at his home in Las Cruces, New Mexico. Inside, the detective penned a simple message, always the same.

Thinking of you.
Jock Collier

CHAPTER 9

Ann Scher was not surprised to hear of her former husband's marriage to Pat Dillon, nor was she upset by it. In the two years since the divorce, her life had changed dramatically. As it turned out, she was planning her own wedding.

Her husband-to-be, John Vitale, was a wealthy man twenty-seven years her senior, the owner of two Ford dealerships in Montrose. A straightforward, jovial man, Vitale had begun to call on Ann shortly after her suicide attempt. He didn't know her well, but he was concerned by what he'd heard around town and he wanted Ann to know she had a friend in him. He, too, had been going through difficult times. His wife of many years had died the previous February, and Vitale was lonely.

At first, Ann felt too bruised to consider a relationship, but John Vitale continued to call her and take

her out to dinner. He was patient with her and kind.
He made her laugh.

At the same time, Ann began seeing a psychologist
who reassured her that she wasn't crazy. She gradually realized that she suffered from low self-esteem
and that she wasn't helpless and stupid the way she'd
felt in her marriage. As Ann regained confidence in
herself and her abilities, she realized that many people
cared for her and were there to help. In time, Stephen
Scher's bitter parting words to her no longer hurt, no
longer mattered. Within a year, she felt well enough
to end treatment.

Meanwhile, her friendship with John Vitale deep-
ened. He didn't manipulate her or lie or cheat. He
was a good man, a loving person. When he asked her
to marry him, Ann said yes.

As part of her divorce settlement from Stephen
Scher, Ann retained the house on the farm and 32
acres of the land. Her new husband wasted no time
in making the place their own. He bought an additional one hundred and forty acres and razed the
house and built a new one. It was a cathartic move
for both of them. Now, nothing remained of the
dwelling where Ann had sunk so low that she'd tried
to end her life. Instead, she decorated her new home
with Vitale's blessings and worked with him at the
car dealership. In stark contrast to the last few years
of her marriage to Scher, her new husband made it
clear that he wanted her by his side. Always.

Ann thanked God many times for her second
chance at happiness. With John Vitale, she felt safe
to share her secrets, to work through the issues that
haunted her from the past. He helped her heal.

Gradually, she began to put the pieces of her past in place. But the legacy of her former marriage would never rest, not in Montrose.

At parties, locals would corner Ann and ask endless questions about her ex-husband: Was there really an affair? Did she actually think he'd killed Marty Dillon?

Ann never knew quite how to respond. Although she believed there had been a physical relationship between her former husband and Pat Dillon, it almost wasn't the point. She often told people that a love affair could mean a lot of things. It could be a vision, an ideal, a wish. It could be two people who barricaded themselves apart emotionally from their spouses, sharing a desire to be together.

Ann was careful to avoid saying anything negative about Pat. She never accused the young nurse of breaking up her marriage—Ann readily admitted that her relationship with Scher was already in trouble by the time Pat entered the picture. In truth, Ann didn't know Pat well. Her only real impression was that Pat had seemed to be a devoted mother.

But Ann did know Stephen Scher. She still believed he had left the pills for her that day when he went out of town with Pat, in hopes that she would take them. She also knew that he was a man who did not hesitate to go after what he wanted, and he wanted Pat Dillon. And so when confronted by others to share her opinion, she did.

"It was his way of arranging the world to suit the way he wanted things to come out," she would say. "It just seemed that if he wanted Pat and there was some difficulty in getting Marty out of the way, he would take advantage of an opportunity to arrange it.''

There were other reasons: all the little untruths that Ann recognized that convinced her even more that Scher lied about what happened at Gunsmoke. Ann felt it when a friend mentioned that Scher had told Jock Collier he had intended to give the Winchester to Marty as a gift.

"He'd never do that," Ann responded without hesitation. "That man was tighter than all get-out. He'd give you something he didn't want anymore, but he wouldn't give up his favorite shotgun."

She reacted the same way when she learned that Scher had smashed the gun against a tree, supposedly in despair. "That's not him," she said. "He was unemotional. He didn't raise his voice, he didn't lose control."

As time passed, it seemed at times as if she was talking about someone else's life, another woman's experience. But now and then a moment would come back to her, a scene from her past, and Ann would remember that Christmas at the Karveller home on Chenango Street, when Pat's mother announced how they'd sent Pat to nursing school in hopes she would marry a doctor. Ann could never forget the uneasy silence that fell in the dining room.

Pat has her doctor now, Ann would think. She wondered if Pat ever considered at what price.

Despite the annual ''greetings'' from Jock Collier, Stephen and Pat Scher managed to put Montrose behind them. They bought a house in Las Cruces, enrolled Michael and Suzanne in Catholic school, and joined a church. Shortly after June 1978 Scher

stopped by a jewelry store to have his wedding band
engraved with Hebrew letters, and he struck up an
animated conversation with the owners, Bill and Susie
Drumm. By the end of the visit, Scher urged Susie
Drumm to meet his new wife.

"You've got to meet Pat," he told her. "She
doesn't know anybody here. You guys would get
along so well."

He was right. The two women immediately hit it
off and became close friends. They shared their pasts,
openly discussing their lives. Pat told Drumm about
the death of her first husband, how Marty had tripped
and fallen on a shotgun, how there were rumors in
town that she and Steve had been having an affair.
Lies, she told Susie Drumm. All lies.

Pat told Susie that she never stopped loving Marty
but that he'd been difficult to live with, prone to mood
swings and depression and terribly controlled by his
father. It was Larry Dillon, Pat charged, who'd driven
the gossip about Steve Scher being responsible for
Marty's death, making it impossible for either one of
them to stay in town. Susie Drumm commiserated
with her new friend. It sounded to her as if the Schers,
through no fault of their own, had suffered enough.

A year after Pat and Stephen Scher married, John
and Laura Karveller sold their house on Chenango
Street in Montrose and relocated to Las Cruces. Then
Pat's brother, Robby, and his wife, Cris, moved west,
too, and Robby got a job running a car dealership in
town. The Karveller family settled in quickly in Las
Cruces. John and Laura became friendly with Susie
Drumm's parents and often socialized as a foursome.

Pat's parents were pleased to see their daughter
happily remarried. To the Karvellers, Stephen Scher

was a perfect mate for Patty. In the months before he left Montrose, he often visited them at their home; Laura Karveller even cooked for him. The Karvellers were convinced that the talk of an affair between the two was ridiculous—their Patty wasn't that kind of girl. The Stephen Scher they knew was kind and thoughtful. He treated Patty's children as if they were his own. And, of course, he was a doctor.

In the fall of 1980, the Scher family grew. At the hospital one night, Stephen Scher learned of a newborn boy whose mother planned to give him up for adoption, and he and Pat quickly decided they wanted the baby. Jonathan was just three days old when they brought him home. By then, Michael was nine, Suzanne, seven. The Dillon children were delighted by their new brother. The baby helped bond them even closer as a family.

The Schers lived well. Stephen Scher drove a high-end steel gray Mercedes he'd bought at an auction, and Pat kept busy with the children, occasionally helping out at her husband's office. Suzanne took voice lessons, like her mother had, and Michael was fascinated by racing, just like his dad. The Schers arranged for a coach, and the young boy began competing in motorcycle races.

In many ways, Stephen Scher appeared to have changed, at least outwardly. Married to the woman he loved, raising three children he embraced as his own, and running a thriving practice, the doctor didn't look back. Even though he was Jewish he attended church with Pat and the children, donating money and giving his time. He became a more approachable physician, was warm to his staff, and developed lasting friendships.

But he couldn't completely escape the past. Back
in Montrose, in her quiet way, Jo Dillon remained
determined to keep in touch with her grandchildren.
She wrote to Michael and Suzanne every Friday on
her lunch hour at Bendix, an airline equipment company where she worked as a secretary. She told them
bits of news about what she and their grandfather
were doing, updates on their cousins and their Aunt
Joann and Uncle Al. Now and then, when Pat sent
photographs or report cards, Jo couldn't have been
more thrilled.

In 1979, three years after Marty's death, Pat Scher
invited Jo Dillon and her former sister-in-law, Joann
Reimel, to Las Cruces for Suzanne's first holy com-
munion. She made it clear that the invitation was not
extended to Larry.

Jo Dillon was beside herself with excitement at seeing her grandchildren again, but the trip was a painful
one. Stephen Scher treated them coldly, and Jo and
Joann were extremely uncomfortable in his presence.
They never returned to Las Cruces again.

Jo continued to send letters, cards, and gifts. On
April 15, 1983, after receiving pictures of the children, she wrote to them: ''You are both beautiful!!!
Sorry, Mike but to grandparents a grandson is equally
as beautiful as a granddaughter, even if boys don't
like such comments. My Christmas present arrived
yesterday and I am so thrilled.''

On another occasion, Jo wrote: ''We are so thrilled
to have pictures of Mike, his bike, the protective
clothing and Suzi snoozing. . . . Our buttons are pop-
ping we are so proud of you both and your accom-

plishments in racing and vocal competition. The pictures and Suzi's report are making the rounds. . . . Wish we could hear you sing, Suzi. (I would probably cry, but grandmothers are allowed weak moments. . . .) Last night we watched motorcycle races from Daytona Beach. It really gives us a good action idea of what you are doing, Mike. The dirt track looked very difficult with the obstacles, etc. Some of the racers looked about your age, Mike. Did your coach ever race at Daytona? I can still see your dad giving you a ride on his motorcycle across the back yards on Kelly Street. So you've been motorcycling a long time!''

In early 1985 Jo described the Christmas holidays to their grandchildren: "Between dinner and dessert Paul and Missy Reimel gave us a piano recital and sing along of Christmas carols. It was a very nice day and we were happy to be with some of our grandchildren. (Miss you both very much.) . . . The spray of evergreen and poinsettias on your Dad's grave is very beautiful. It shows up nicely with or without snow.''

Later that year, in Montrose, Jock Collier retired. The sixty-seven-year-old detective had still not lost faith that the Scher case would one day be tried. He discussed it with the incoming county detective, Frank Bayer.

"I want to show you this case," Jock told him. "I want you to know about it." He showed Bayer the memo he had written almost a decade earlier and said he believed that the day would come, that someday, someone would listen and prosecute Stephen Scher for murder.

The following year, at a dedication ceremony for the new Pennsylvania state police barracks, Jock introduced himself to Corporal Richard Kane, the new chief crime officer. At Collier's urging, Kane agreed to pull the Dillon file and review it. Collier felt hopeful for the first time in years. He planned to follow up with Kane and make sure the corporal kept his promise.

But soon after, on Christmas Eve 1986, Jock Collier wasn't well. During the day, he drove his wife, Alice, to the hairdresser and waited in the car. That evening, the couple dropped by their son's home, but they left early so Jock could rest. At ten o'clock Alice Collier called her son to say that something terrible was wrong with Jock.

Ken Fisher found his stepfather collapsed in shock in an armchair, his head rolled back, arms outstretched. On the coffee table was a medical dictionary, the page open to the section on blood disorders. Jock was rushed to Lourdes Hospital in Binghamton, but he died the next morning—of a blood disorder.

The irony wasn't lost on Ken. It was just like Jock, Ken thought, to figure out exactly what was wrong.

At Jock's funeral, hundreds came to pay their respects. The caravan of cars was so long it stretched from downtown Susquehanna to the cemetery several miles away. Alice Collier was touched by the display of admiration for her husband.

"I knew everyone loved him," she told her son Ken. "I just didn't know he knew so many people."

Among the mourners was Larry Dillon. He was saddened to lose a friend; at the same time he was crushed that his strongest supporter was gone. Over the years, Jock's tenacity had bolstered Larry's spirits.

On one level, Larry Dillon knew there was still a chance that the case might one day be investigated. In the fall of 1985, after he had left the car agency and gone to work part time for Bartron's Funeral Home, Larry ended up transporting a body to an autopsy with Frank Zanin, the records and identification officer who'd been to Gunsmoke. On the drive, the officer told him that he always believed Marty's death had been a homicide. The officer went on to disclose that the case had technically never been closed. The evidence—the broken gun, the spent cartridge, the bloody tree stump, and the photos were still in a storage locker at the barracks. Even the clothes and boots that Jock Collier had collected from Dr. Scher were still intact, along with a copy of the statement Scher gave to the detective on June 4.

So it was all there, waiting for someone to take action.

But as time passed, Larry Dillon began to feel as if he'd reached the end of his struggle. With Jock, there had been a chance. Alone, he felt helpless.

For the next two years, Larry and Jo Dillon prayed for an answer. They asked that God send someone to help them, so at last, before they died, they might know the truth about what happened at Gunsmoke.

There was one such person, just as determined as Jock Collier, strong enough to pick up where the detective left off and to do what Jo and Larry Dillon couldn't.

Her name was Bonnie Mead.

CHAPTER 10

For almost a decade, Bonnie Mead had been working as a secretary for Larry Kelly at the law firm
he and his brother, Paul, ran on Public Avenue. She'd
stayed just three years at Bob Dean's after Marty
died. The office hadn't been the same without the
young lawyer. Bob Dean, in particular, was crushed
by the loss—Marty had been like a son to him. A
melancholy haze settled on the staff, and finally, Bonnie left. The atmosphere had become too depressing.

Not long after Bonnie joined the Kellys, Ed Little's
term as district attorney ran out, and Larry Kelly was
elected to the part-time post. By 1988, though, Larry
Kelly was back to private practice, and a new Susquehanna County DA, Jeffrey Snyder, was sworn in.

In the fall of that year, Bonnie came up with an
idea. Kelly & Kelly took on a civil case, representing
a woman badly injured after a car veered into her
lane, causing a crash that killed two people. Larry

Kelly hired W. Stewart Bennett, a former New York state trooper, to analyze the accident. It was Bennett's job to determine the speed of the vehicle and to reconstruct how the crash had occurred.

By studying various pieces of evidence, including the size and shape of blood spatter found on the car, Bennett was able to compile a comprehensive explanation. Armed with Bennett's report, Larry Kelly ultimately negotiated a large settlement from the driver's insurance company.

In November of 1988, when the case was over, Larry Kelly and Stew Bennett stopped into Bonnie Mead's office for a chat. Bonnie Mead turned to her boss. "I want to ask you something. What do you think about Stew looking at Marty Dillon's case? Could he tell Larry Dillon what happened? That way, we could all put it to rest."

Before Larry Kelly could reply, Stew cut in. "Sure I could. I can't promise Larry Dillon it's going to be what he wants to hear. But physical evidence doesn't lie. We can certainly tell what happened."

As soon as she got home from work that night, Bonnie Mead phoned Marty's sister Joann Reimel. Bonnie explained about Stew Bennett, whom Joann said she recalled from high school, where they'd been in the same class. Bonnie told Joann about the case the firm had been handling, how Bennett had been able to assess a great deal about an accident from examining the evidence. She asked if the Dillon family would be interested in hiring Bennett to figure out what really happened at Gunsmoke.

Joann immediately gave Bonnie her parents' phone number at the hunting camp and asked the secretary to please repeat everything she'd just said to Larry and Jo Dillon.

Minutes later, Bonnie was on the phone with Larry Dillon. By the time she finished speaking, Marty's father was weeping softly.

"You're the answer to our prayers," he told Bonnie Mead. "We've waited for this ever since Jock died. We prayed someone would call and help us."

The Dillons arranged to meet with Stew Bennett after the holidays. The investigator told them he was confident he could determine what had happened to Marty but warned the couple that they should prepare themselves for a range of possibilities. "You'll have to accept what I find, one way or another," he told them.

Larry and Jo Dillon agreed. They told Bennett that all they ever wanted was to know the truth.

It was a turning point in their lives. For the first time there was something the Dillons could do, someone who had a strategy. At the same time, they were keenly aware that their grandchildren would soon graduate from high school. The children, they reasoned, were now old enough to deal with the questions surrounding their father's death. Larry and Jo Dillon were hopeful that Michael and Suzanne would support their efforts to learn the truth.

The Dillons gathered what they could for Stew Bennett. Larry gave the investigator the copy of Scher's statement that Jock Collier had given him years earlier. He also asked John Conarton for copies of the autopsy report, as well as the photos.

As for Bonnie Mead, she was pleased she'd been able to introduce the Dillons to Stew Bennett and was so energized she wanted to help even more. She turned to her longtime boyfriend, Tom Sivahop, a state trooper from Wilkes-Barre, for advice. Over the years, she'd occasionally tried to bring up the circumstances around Marty Dillon's death, but Sivahop hadn't been particularly receptive. He told her he had enough police work on the job; at home he just wanted to relax.

This time, Bonnie forced him to listen. When she was done explaining about the events of June 2, 1976, Tom Sivahop was stunned. He was an accomplished hunter as well as an experienced trooper, and he was convinced it wasn't possible for the victim to have tripped and fallen on a shotgun the way Scher had said. He was also aware that a number 4 magnum would never be used for skeet shooting. From what Bonnie said, he realized, too, that there was a possible motive for homicide.

Sivahop told Bonnie that he would call Richard Kane, the head of the crime unit at the Dunmore Barracks of the state police. Though they were assigned to different troops, Sivahop had known Kane for years and respected the corporal. He spoke to him by phone a short time later.

"Rich, have you ever stumbled on the Dillon investigation?" Sivahop asked.

"As a matter of fact," Kane said, "I have it right here."

The corporal explained that Jock Collier had brought it to his attention a couple of years before. The file had been sitting on his desk for some time.

"Rich, this individual was blown away," Sivahop continued. "This is indicative of murder."

Corporal Kane did not disagree and admitted that because of the lingering questions surrounding the death, the evidence was still kept in a locker at the barracks. Sivahop asked why the case wasn't being looked at, and Kane confessed that the police investigators back then had done almost nothing. The file, he explained, contained only a copy of Scher's statement to Jock Collier and a 1976 FBI report confirming that there was human blood on Dr. Scher's boots.

"The report is so minute I have nothing to go on," Kane told him. "I have nothing to work with. If you could give me anything substantial to go on, I'd be more than happy to run with it."

Tom Sivahop took Corporal Kane's suggestion seriously. He called Don and Susan Strope from the ambulance crew and Bob Elliott and Jerry Thorne, the game protectors who'd been among the first at the scene. He told all of them he was not assigned to work on the case, he was simply gathering information to assist in possibly opening an investigation. Sivahop had been with the state police long enough to know that he needed to be very careful not to overstep his authority. It was especially sensitive, he realized, because he didn't even work in the troop that would ordinarily have jurisdiction.

When Sivahop reached Bob Elliott, the game protector told him he would be happy to talk to investigators. After the trooper said someone would be in touch with him soon, Bob Elliott shrugged. "I've been waiting for twelve years. I won't hold my breath."

Next, Sivahop called District Attorney Jeff Snyder and asked if he would meet with the Dillons, and the DA agreed. Sivahop then phoned Jock Collier's widow, Alice, and asked if the detective had left any papers or photos from the case.

His hopes were dashed. The elderly woman admitted that just six months earlier, she'd burned all of Jock's files. "I didn't want anything to get into the wrong hands," she explained.

Tom Sivahop decided that his next step was to approach Lieutenant George Kamage of Troop R in Dunmore. He reasoned that if he could interest both Kane and Kamage in the case, it might spur an investigation faster.

"No way in the world this man blew himself away," Sivahop told Kamage. "George, get a shotgun. I'll show you. It's impossible to commit suicide with that shotgun. There was motive—the doctor was running with his wife. Look, I've talked to Rich Kane—they have everything, all the evidence, a pile of stuff."

Sivahop went on to say that he'd put together a list of people who were willing to be interviewed. He told Kamage he planned to give the names to Kane.

That night, Sivahop told Bonnie about the meeting he'd had. They thought it sounded a little promising.

But less than a week later, Tom Sivahop was summoned to Kamage's office. The lieutenant closed the door and silently handed him a letter sharply rebuking his efforts the previous week. The missive ended harshly:

"In the future you will refrain from any personal involvement in this investigation. . . . Any statement you may make concerning the guilt or innocence of any involved party are made at your own peril."

Sivahop was shocked. He said nothing as Lieutenant Kamage went on to inform him that he should forget about this case.

Tom Sivahop realized that he was embroiled in a precarious situation. He got the list from Bonnie and gave it to Kane. Then he told Bonnie that from that point on he had to steer clear of the case. Lieutenant Kamage's letter had made that clear.

But Tom Sivahop and Bonnie Mead weren't giving up. They would find a way.

CHAPTER II

A few weeks after Sivahop's request, District Attorney Jeff Snyder spent three hours in the living room of 27 Lincoln Avenue taking copious notes as Larry and Jo Dillon, Joann and Alan Reimel, and Bonnie Mead voiced their concerns regarding Marty's death. When he left, the group felt some hope. The DA seemed genuinely interested in what they had to say.

Over the next three months, Snyder and the state police did a cursory investigation, visiting the site at Gunsmoke and examining the evidence in the barracks.

At the end of April, the DA, Corporal Kane, Lieutenant Kamage, and Frank Zanin drove to the University of Pennsylvania for a presentation to a gathering of twenty-nine medical examiners and forensic pathologists. Among them was Dr. Isadore Mihalakis, a leading forensic pathologist from Lehigh

University Medical Center in Allentown. Mihalakis had consulted with John Conarton back in 1976, when the coroner called to ask what to look for in an accidental shooting.

Snyder and his group had little to show the medical experts—only Dr. Grace's slim autopsy report, Scher's account of the accident, and a few photographs.

Yet by a show of hands, Dr. Mihalakis later testified, a majority of the specialists agreed that the manner of death had been a homicide. A smaller number chose suicide or accident.

Yet, inexplicably, a month later, Jeff Snyder called the Dillons and told them the reverse. He said of the twenty-nine, only twelve voted for homicide, while seventeen believed the manner of death to have been an accident or suicide. The DA then followed up his conversation with the couple in writing. In a letter dated May 24, 1989, DA Snyder offered little optimism that criminal charges would ever be brought against Stephen Scher.

> *Overwhelmingly, the medical experts concluded that the manner of death was either accidentally or intentionally self inflicted. I must inform you that in my opinion my predecessors in office acted correctly in finding insufficient grounds to proceed with any criminal prosecution. Unfortunately the passage of time only creates greater difficulties for most prosecutions, and in this matter a thirteen year interim renders it a virtual impossibility short of anything less than a confession. As District Attorney, I will not approve any criminal complaint in this*

matter. The State Police, will, of course, act upon any new information which may become available in the future. Copy of this letter will be kept at the Susquehanna County District Attorney's Office, and copy will be provided to the Pennsylvania State Police so that some institutional history of this review is maintained and can be reviewed if deemed appropriate by my successors in office.

No one else can truly share your pain suffered at the loss of your son. I know your pain still exists today. I sincerely express my sympathies to you for your loss.

Snyder's letter devastated the Dillons, but this time, Bonnie Mead was there to buoy their spirits, just the way Jock had years before. She reminded them that Stew Bennett was preparing to start experimenting with ballistics at his home office in Silver Lake. He intended to re-create the size of the bullet wound in Marty's body to determine the shotgun's distance and angle.

Besides, the Dillons had an important event to look forward to—Michael and Suzanne were coming to Montrose for the first time since 1978. Both of the Dillon children were graduating from high school that spring—Suzanne had completed an accelerated program and was graduating at the same time as her older brother—and the Dillons had sent plane tickets as a gift. Since their son's death, Larry and Jo had seen Michael and Suzanne just once before, when the Schers vacationed on the beach in Ocean City, New Jersey, and the Dillons drove down for the evening and took their grandchildren to dinner.

This visit was special. To the Dillons, their grand-children were finally coming home.

The trip went well. The Dillons gave Michael and Suzanne a tour of Montrose and took them to Gun-smoke. To Larry and Jo's surprise, however, their grandchildren declined the offer to visit their father's grave. But they did go to 7 Kelly Street, and Suzanne spent time with Michelle Lewis, whose parents had bought the house from Pat and who was just Suz-anne's age. Michelle showed her new friend her bed-room, which had once been Suzanne's, thirteen years previously.

It was hard to say good-bye. As their son's children walked through the gate at the airport, waving, Larry and Jo wondered what the future held—for all of them.

By mid-July of that year, Stew Bennett was engrossed in ballistics testing, and Bonnie Mead and Tom Siva-hop stopped by one afternoon to observe his work. Us-ing the same make and model Winchester, Bennett shot into pigskin to attempt to simulate the same-size wound found in Dillon's chest. The investigator ulti-mately had to retreat three to five feet away to create a hole 1¼ inches. Bennett later shared his findings with two forensic pathologists. In the end, all agreed: It was impossible for the shooting to have been an accident.

Larry Dillon was not surprised to hear Bennett's conclusion. Later that summer, he and his son-in-law, Al Reimel, went to see Dr. Grace, who performed the autopsy on Marty, and asked him to meet with Stew Bennett to share any information he had. At one point, Dr. Grace unabashedly told the two that he thought Marty had used poor judgment in going shooting alone with Scher.

Marty Dillon and son Michael, then 3, in 1974.
(Photo: Larry and Jo Dillon)

The woods at Gunsmoke where Marty Dillon was murdered on June 2, 1976. (*Photo: April Saul*)

Marty Dillon and his prized BMW shortly before his death.
(*Photo: Bonnie Mead*)

Ann and Stephen Scher were all smiles following their 1963 wedding in Michigan.
(Photo: courtesy Ann Vitale)

Stephen Scher, flanked by his wife Pat and then attorney Peter O'Malley, at a press conference following the coroner's ruling of homicide. Scher denied having an affair with Pat and called Marty Dillon his best friend. (*Photo: Rich Banick)*

Patricia Dillon Scher, with son Michael (second from left), and daughter Suzanne enters court on the first day of her husband's trial in her hometown of Montrose, Pa. (*AP photo/Chris Gardner)*

Above: Dr. Stephen Scher, center, and his wife Patricia Dillon Scher, walk into the Susquehanna County Court of Common Pleas with attorney John Moses before closing arguments in Scher's murder trial, Tuesday, Oct. 21, 1997, in Montrose, Pa. *(AP Photo/Chris Gardner)*

Left: Senior Deputy Attorney General Robert Campolongo near the end of the seven-week trial. *(AP Photo/Chris Gardner)*

"I'm so relieved but I have no joy because we've lost our grand-children," Jo Dillon, with her husband Larry, told reporters after the verdict.

(Photo credit: Dave Kennedy, Binghamton Press & Sun Bulletin)

Cheers erupted from the crowd as Stephen Scher was led to jail.
At right is Sheriff Dick Pelicci.
(Photo: Rich Banick)

Joann Reimel, Marty Dillon's sister, visits his grave at the Holy Name of Mary Cemetery.
(Photo: April Saul)

A few weeks later, the Dillons asked John Conarton to come to their home. The coroner knew that the Dillons had hired Stew Bennett. Earlier that year, he'd spoken briefly to him.

"It was an accident," Conarton insisted to Bennett. "You'll never change my mind."

At the Dillons' house, Conarton was less brash. Jo, who'd begun to keep a diary of their efforts, later wrote that the coroner acted nervous throughout the visit. "I think he has a problem with his conscience," she wrote.

Larry Dillon told John Conarton that they were not satisfied with the circumstances surrounding Marty's death. The coroner said he was surprised—he thought the Dillons had accepted his ruling. Conarton explained how he thought the accident had happened: Marty tripping over his shoelace, dropping the gun, the Winchester goes off. The shoelace was untied, after all. Conarton had seen it himself. He reminded the couple that there was even a photo of it.

Larry Dillon used a walking stick to demonstrate on the coroner that it couldn't have happened that way. He asked John Conarton to meet with Stew Bennett; he said that the investigator had more questions. Conarton agreed but ended up postponing the meeting repeatedly until almost the end of the year.

In January 1990, a year after he'd been hired, Stew Bennett pulled everything together in a report. It had taken him much longer to do the work because of the trouble he'd had getting all the information from the various sources. In the end, however, his judgment was firm—Marty Dillon's death had been a homicide.

Bennett sent a copy of his report to Major Michael Jordan of the Pennsylvania state police. By now, the

Dillons had a surprising new supporter: John Conarton. After he'd finally talked to Bennett and read the report, the coroner changed his mind.

Conarton went to see DA Snyder and also paid a visit to the Gibson Barracks. But the state police continued to move slowly. After much discussion, in the spring of 1990, it was decided that Corporal Richard Kane would approach Dr. Scher in New Mexico and attempt to have him sign the statement he'd given to Jock Collier in 1976. At the same time, Kane would request a more in-depth interview.

The corporal flew to Las Cruces in April and went directly to meet with members of the Las Cruces police. Then, two officers from the department accompanied Kane to Dr. Scher's allergy office.

When the corporal identified himself to the receptionist in the waiting room, Dr. Stephen Scher, upon hearing the news, barricaded himself in the back and called attorney Peter O'Malley in Pennsylvania at once.

"I have two police officers in my waiting room," the doctor said urgently. "They want to interview me."

O'Malley told him to put the corporal on the phone. The attorney was furious. "I resent you going behind my back," O'Malley barked at Kane. "I could have saved you about a five-thousand-mile round-trip if you had the courtesy to call me. Now, what are you doing there and what do you want?"

Corporal Kane explained that he had an unsigned statement that the doctor had given in 1976. The state police wanted his signature and an opportunity to ask more questions.

Not surprisingly, O'Malley told him Scher

wouldn't sign or say anything. "You come back to Pennsylvania and you send me a copy of that statement," he told Kane. "I will review it and make a determination whether the doctor will sign it."

He told the corporal he was on private property and to leave immediately. As a finishing touch, O'Malley threatened to alert the press. "If I can't get you arrested out there, at least I can get you on the front page of the Las Cruces newspaper for trespassing," the attorney warned.

Back in Montrose, Larry and Jo Dillon expected that Pat would be livid to learn of the visit from the state police. But three months later, in July 1990, Pat called the Dillons to tell them that Michael's close friend, Alicia, had died of a brain tumor, and the young man was distraught. She mentioned nothing about the state police.

Jo Dillon noted in her diary her surprise: *We think Pat doesn't know*, she wrote. Two months later, Pat called again, to give an update on the children. Michael was doing well racing motorcycles professionally. Suzanne had just started as a freshman at Colorado College in Colorado Springs. Again, nothing was said about the visit.

Around the same time, Joann Reimel wrote to Major Jordan, asking for a status report. He told her someone would contact her soon.

A month later, she called again and said no one had been in touch. It wasn't until the end of the year that the Dillons and Reimels were at last able to set up an appointment with Lieutenant Kamage and Corporal Kane. At that meeting, the two men admitted that they now believed that Marty's death had been a homicide. They also told the family that they both would be retiring the following year but reassured them that the investigation would continue.

In January 1991, Joann wrote to Pennsylvania State Attorney General Ernest Preate, asking him to look into the case. A few weeks later, Bonnie Mead suggested that the Dillons attend a dinner sponsored by the Susquehanna County Republican Committee, where Preate was to be the guest of honor.

At the cocktail party, Bonnie arranged an introduction, and Preate listened to Larry Dillon's account of their story. The attorney general promised to get back to them.

Two days later, Joann Reimel, overwhelmed by frustration, called Major Jordan and broke into tears. She'd had it with officials who made promises and commitments they never seemed to keep. In recent months she and her parents had asked the state police repeatedly who was going to oversee the investigation after Kane and Kamage retired, and they never got any answers.

She asked Major Jordan how he would feel if his son was murdered today and no one was willing to investigate it.

Jordan tried to reassure her that they were taking the case seriously, but Joann Reimel was inconsolable. "We've been having the fight of our lives for two years with the state police," she told him bitterly.

"Don't say that," the major soothed. He promised to look into the delay.

Joann hung up, exasperated. She'd heard that too many times before.

It wasn't until three months later, in May 1991, that the state police finally sent evidence to the FBI lab in

Quantico, Virginia. When the report came back, the news was staggering. The boots contained high-velocity blood spatter, revealing that the wearer had been within a few feet of the victim. The report also stated that the spatter on the tree stump and on the instep of Dillon's shoe suggested that he may have been sitting or squatting near the log, not running. Ballistics experts had reassembled Scher's broken shotgun and test-fired it, determining the muzzle was up to three feet away when it was fired—almost exactly what Stew Bennett had said several years earlier.

In Las Cruces, Dr. Stephen Scher knew nothing of the goings-on in Montrose. In his mind, his secret was still safe, buried deep in the ground. To be sure, the visit from Corporal Kane undoubtedly rattled him, but Stephen Scher had developed a remarkable ability to go on, to live his life without fear of retribution for the sins of his past.

He didn't know it, but the drumbeat of the forest at Gunsmoke was growing louder.

CHAPTER 12

By the summer of 1991, Stephen and Pat Scher were preparing to leave Las Cruces. In recent years, gangs from nearby Mexico had begun to infiltrate the area, and crime in the city was on the rise. Concerned about Jonathan, then almost eleven years old, the Schers decided to relocate. They made arrangements to lease space to another physician in order to keep the allergy practice in Las Cruces running.

The timing seemed right. Michael Dillon was spending most of his time on the road, racing professionally, and Suzanne was happy studying fashion design in Colorado. Robby Karveller, Pat's brother, was settled in Las Cruces, running an auto dealership. He would look after Laura Karveller, now a widow. John Karveller had passed away unexpectedly several years earlier, just weeks before what would have been the couple's fiftieth wedding anniversary.

Through an agency that matched physicians with

hospitals in need of certain specialities, the Schers
started their search, at one point considering an offer
from a hospital in Washington. Scher had flown there
for a visit but ultimately declined the offer. Then, in
the spring of 1992, the agent told Scher about Lincolnton, North Carolina, near Charlotte.

It sounded ideal. Six months earlier the area's previous physician, who had served the community for
thirty years, had retired after undergoing open-heart
surgery. The community, small yet growing, was in
dire need of a family practitioner. The Charlotte Airport was a main hub for US Airways, making it easy
to travel back and forth to Las Cruces.

Stephen Scher flew to Lincolnton in April, and the
hospital's administrator, Ken Wehunt, met him at the
airport. Wehunt was anxious to make a good impression. He showed Scher around the hospital and introduced him to about ten physicians at a small reception
hosted by the board of directors. Wehunt then accompanied Scher to inspect a newly renovated office on
Dave Warlick Drive, just a few blocks away, where
Scher could open his practice. Later, Wehunt took his
visitor for a drive around town, answering questions
about the school districts and passing several houses
for sale. At one point, the administrator slowed down
in front of a sprawling brick split level for sale, less
than a mile from the hospital, but Dr. Scher immediately dismissed it. ''Pat wouldn't like that,'' he said.
''That's too cold looking.''

As Scher got a feel for the area, Ken Wehunt was
sizing him up as well. He found the doctor a bit distant, but Scher was forthright and Ken liked that about
him. He's plain spoken, Wehunt thought.

That evening, several physicians from the hospital

joined Scher and Wehunt for dinner at a restaurant
overlooking Lake Norman. The doctors spoke highly
of their practices in Lincolnton and about the medical
facility.

Scher was amenable to the package the hospital
offered. For the first two years, in order to build up
his practice, he'd have free rent in the new office and
a guaranteed salary of $12,000 a month.

Over the next two months, Scher visited Lincolnton
at least three times, and Pat came on several occasions
as well. As it turned out, Scher was mistaken—Pat
loved the corner brick house.

When Wehunt joined the doctor and a realtor to
tour the inside, the doctor bluntly gave his opinion.
"Why in the world would anyone put this chickenshit
brown carpet all over the house?" he asked.

The realtor was taken aback, but Wehunt wasn't.
By now, he understood the doctor a bit better. Plain
spoken, Wehunt thought.

Over the summer of 1992, Larry and Jo Dillon
learned from their grandson, Michael Dillon, of the
Schers' move. In July, the Dillons drove several hours
to Hagerstown, Maryland, to watch Michael compete
on a Harley-Davidson at the Camel Pro AMA, bringing along Joann Reimel's youngest son, Matthew.
When the race was over, Michael returned with his
grandparents to Montrose for several days.

The Dillons were delighted to spend time with their
grandson. At one point during the visit Larry Dillon
managed to ask Michael if he'd received the insurance money from his father's policy, and the young
man said he had, that the money had been invested
for him and his sister. Michael told his grandparents

he had recently bought a house in Las Cruces with his share of the inheritance.

In August of 1992, when Stephen, Pat, and Jonathan Scher moved to Lincolnton, the hospital board paid the agency a $20,000 fee for referring the doctor. They considered it money well spent. Scher opened his office on Dave Warlick Drive and hired a staff. The local newspaper, the *Lincoln Times,* published a story about his arrival, and patients began calling to set up appointments. Once a month for a few days Scher commuted to Las Cruces to work in his original office. Financially, the Schers were doing quite well.

They settled in quickly. Within a short time, Dr. Scher was invited to join Wehunt and several physicians in the hospital cafeteria for coffee every morning after rounds. The doctors liked Scher. He seemed professional and committed to his work. Wehunt heard mostly good reports from Scher's patients, and the hospital administrator was pleased. In a short time, Wehunt began to use Dr. Scher to help recruit other medical personnel. Scher told visitors that Lincolnton was a great place to work.

A month after their arrival, the Schers joined the one-room shingled St. Dorothy's Catholic Church, about three miles from downtown in the western tip of Lincolnton. The Reverend Richard Farwell welcomed them warmly. The priest, ordained in 1981, had served as a monk for ten years before becoming pastor of the Hickory, North Carolina, church and ultimately transferring to St. Dorothy's in the early 1990s. The church had a membership of about 150 families.

From the start, the priest was not shy about admitting that he took notice when a professional couple moved to town. Fund-raising, Farwell believed, was a crucial foundation for any religious organization. Within a few months after the Schers' arrival, Fallwell approached them about donating money toward a new organ. The Schers wrote a $1,000 check without hesitation.

A year later, during St. Dorothy's campaign to build a new church, the Schers were even more generous, giving $2,000 in memory of some of their relatives. At other times, Pat and Steve paid for new stained-glass windows with images of St. Jude.

The priest was delighted by his new parishioners. They attended mass regularly, even joining an evangelism program called Renew in which they met with about fifteen other congregants for prayer services weekly for two years. The Schers enrolled Jonathan in Sunday School, and the boy also participated in the youth ministry program on Sunday evenings. Pat volunteered as a team member for the program on a retreat. The couple continued to respect Stephen Scher's religious heritage—on Passover, the Schers even invited Reverend Farwell to their home for a seder.

The Schers were clearly happy in their new home. "We'll never go anyplace else," Pat confided in her new friends. "We just love the people here."

But five hundred miles away, the drumbeat continued. There had been some setbacks in the past year— in February 1992 John Conarton died undergoing surgery for cancer, and eleven months later Dr. Grace, too, died of cancer—but the state police reassured the Dillons that the deaths wouldn't derail a prosecution. Throughout most of 1993 the state police waited for more detailed FBI reports. At the end of the year, Major Jordan acknowledged to the Dillons that the case against Stephen Scher deserved to be put before a jury.

By now it had been five years since the Dillons and Bonnie Mead began their push. It was almost time.

CHAPTER 13

Two important events occurred in 1994: Justine Jenner, the woman whom Scher had asked about the tenets of Catholicism, wrote a letter to Larry and Jo Dillon revealing the doctor's questions to her a few weeks before the shooting. And Tom Scales, a Pennsylvania state police sergeant with no ties to the case, grew so impatient that he did his own investigation, writing a blistering twenty-four-page report detailing compelling evidence against Dr. Stephen Scher.

Justine Jenner's disclosure came as a total surprise; she'd never told anyone but her husband about the conversation she'd had with Stephen Scher. But in early 1994 she'd been quite ill for more than five months and was worried she might die. Although they were neighbors, Justine Jenner didn't know the Dillons well, but she'd heard of the couple's struggle to get the state police to investigate their son's death. She decided she had to step forward.

"I have to tell," she told her husband. "It's a secret that shouldn't be a secret. I have to get it off my conscience."

At her home just across the street from the Dillons, Jenner took a yellow tablet and wrote about the day in 1976 when Scher visited. She disclosed that Scher had wanted to know what would happen if he took Patty out of town, if she would still be able to practice her religion. In the letter, she apologized to the Dillons for holding back the information for so long. She confessed that she had been so very fond of Dr. Scher that she hadn't wanted to cause him any trouble.

Even after receiving Justine Jenner's letter, the investigation continued to drag. By now, Tom Sivahop was thoroughly disgusted by the delay. He suggested that Bonnie call Tom Scales, a seasoned investigator at the Gibson Barracks, with a reputation for getting things done.

On his own, Sergeant Scales did what his colleagues within the department had not for all these years—he interviewed witnesses. He talked to the game protectors and to Justine Jenner. He then got hold of the Dillon file, including the FBI findings, and compiled a report. With the evidence of blood spatter, the distance of the shotgun, and the size and shape of the wound, Scales definitively stated that the death of Martin Dillon was no accident and a thorough investigation should be ordered at once.

Tom Scales's presumptive move was not well received by his superiors. He was chastised for interfering and immediately reassigned to administrative

duties. He fought back, hiring an attorney from Waverly, Peter Loftus, and threatening to bring charges
against the department. In the end, a transfer for the
sergeant was authorized with no reprimand.

Ultimately, though, Tom Scales succeeded. He
shook the complacent department heads, alerted the
police commissioner to the case, and energized the
Dillons into taking action. By the winter of 1994, yet
another person was named to take over the investigation, Lieutenant Frank Hacken, the newly promoted
chief of the crime unit at Dunmore. Hacken, too,
promised the Dillons a thorough examination of the
case, but by this point, Larry and Jo were done waiting.

At Bonnie Mead's urging, the Dillons hired
Scales's attorney, Peter Loftus, in June 1994, eighteen
years after the death of their son. A month later, on
July 19, they filed a petition on their own for exhumation in the Court of Common Pleas Criminal Division. That evening, Larry Dillon stood on the steps
of the Susquehanna County courthouse facing an array of television cameras and stated that Marty's
death had been murder and that the family was demanding a reautopsy. Legal papers were to be served
to Pat Dillon Scher, as Marty's widow, requesting the
release of the body.

There was no turning back. Pat's relatives in the
area saw Larry Dillon on the evening news and immediately notified the Schers in Lincolnton. The following morning, at seven, a furious Pat called Joann
Reimel. "Why are you doing this?" she asked, crying. "Have you no regard for the children?"

Pat went on to accuse the Dillons of trying to ruin
her husband's career, complaining that the press at-

tention was going to damage his practice and that Jonathan was going to be hurt. She was enraged about the effects of the Dillons' allegations on Michael and Suzanne. "You're pitting my children against me," she charged.

At first, Joann was taken aback to hear from her former sister-in-law and listened silently for a few minutes. Then, Joann interrupted her. "Pat, we've had the ultimate—Marty dying," she said simply. "This is all secondary."

"I guess I'm not going to get anywhere with you, Joann," Pat retorted and hung up the phone.

There was one aspect of their struggle to learn the truth that Larry and Jo Dillon did not anticipate: the bitter reaction of Michael and Suzanne Dillon.

Naively, the Dillons had expected that the children would want to know what really happened at Gunsmoke. Instead, their son's children, astonished by accusations they'd heard nothing about previously, felt betrayed by their grandparents and instantly united behind their stepfather. He had raised them, and they loved him. Not for a moment would they believe he would ever have committed murder.

Michael called his grandparents once, demanding to know why they were doing this, but hung up in anger when Jo Dillon, meeting with the state police at the time, told him she had visitors and would explain later. Jo tried writing to the children and continued to send checks on their birthdays, but always the letters were returned, unopened, and the checks uncashed.

It was painful, but by now the Dillons had endured so much they continued to keep faith in God that they were doing the right thing. They visited Marty's grave almost daily, as they had for years, and prayed at the spot at Gunsmoke where he'd died, now marked with an iron cross. They hoped that one day their grandchildren would understand.

Pat Scher hired Peter O'Malley to fight the Dillons' exhumation petition in court and retained Dr. John Shane, chief of pathology at Lehigh University Medical Center in Allentown, as an expert. Meanwhile, the Dillons' lawyer, Peter Loftus, started taking depositions from various witnesses regarding Dr. Stephen Scher.

One of them was Ann Vitale. During the summer of 1994, she spent several hours in the attorney's office, chronicling her life with Scher. Ann told the attorney about their courtship and the early years of the marriage and tried to recount how their relationship had come undone. She detailed his treatment of her, how he'd admitted to being in love with Pat, the pills he'd left for her, how he'd flatly confessed that he'd shot Shadow, their dog.

Then, Larry and Jo Dillon asked Ann to come to Gunsmoke. She went with Bonnie Mead. They all stood by the cross, the marker where Marty Dillon had died.

"If you're going to help us," Larry Dillon told Ann, "you need to know. This is the spot. This is what we believe happened."

As Larry talked, Ann listened intently. She'd initially felt a bit nervous when she heard that the Dillons wanted to see her. Over the years, she'd passed them in town but had never spoken more than a greeting to them. That day at Gunsmoke she found herself impressed by the couple's fortitude. They were very matter-of-fact, she thought. Not emotionally charged at all.

"I don't know how they can stand this up and down, this roller-coaster ride," she told her husband later that night.

Ann then warned John Vitale that if she was ultimately called to testify against Stephen Scher, her involvement in the case could affect their car dealership business. Vitale told her not to worry about it. "You do what you have to do."

By the fall of 1994 it was clear that the Dillons' attempt to exhume their son's body was going nowhere. As parents, they had a lesser legal standing than Pat, the widow. But the attention to the case was growing, and that, the Dillons knew, continuously put pressure on the state police.

Larry Dillon gave several interviews to the local press. On one occasion, he brought P. J. Amadio, a reporter for the *Scranton Times,* to Gunsmoke.

"My son knew firearms," he told the reporter. "I taught him how to use them, I taught him to respect them. There's no way he would run through the woods, trip, and kill himself."

In November of 1994 Bonnie Mead suggested that all the supporters of the Dillons gather at a community meeting in Montrose, sponsored by Major Michael Jordan of the Pennsylvania state police. Channel 16, the Scranton station, would be there, as well as a reporter for the *Susquehanna County Independent.* This was a good opportunity, Bonnie told everyone, to put even more pressure on the state police.

The night of the meeting, friends of the Dillons

filled the room. The game protectors showed up, and so did Ann Vitale and Elaine Petrzala, the secretary who'd taken Scher's statement to Jock Collier.

The group split apart and sat scattered throughout the room. When Major Jordan arrived to open the meeting, he was clearly uncomfortable to find the Dillons, the Reimels, and Bonnie Mead in the front row. Before the question-and-answer portion of the evening began, Jordan requested that Bonnie and the Dillons not ask any questions about the case; he promised to meet with them privately as soon as the meeting ended.

They paid no attention. During the meeting, a friend of Larry and Jo's asked what was holding up the Dillon case.

"I can't talk about an ongoing investigation," Jordan said.

The major's response was greeted by laughter from the crowd.

Then, Jo Dillon's cousin, Bill Nash, raised his hand. "We're the family," he called out, "and we don't see any activity on the case."

Jordan sighed. He repeated that he couldn't discuss the case now, but he promised again to meet with the group privately at the end of the meeting.

He did. The Dillons and their supporters circled him, firing questions for almost twenty minutes.

"It doesn't appear you've been doing much of anything," Bonnie Mead announced.

"You lied," Joann Reimel charged. "You always say you're doing things and you don't."

In the end, Major Jordan swore he would look into the delay and find out why things had been moving so slowly.

The next day, he called Bonnie Mead at work. He

told her how embarrassed he was about the previous evening and that he was going to assign two officers to the case.

By the end of the year, Lieutenant Frank Hacken was given the go-ahead to choose two troopers to work full time on the Dillon case. The lieutenant considered his choices and picked Steve Stoud, who'd transferred to the Gibson Barracks just six months earlier, and Jamie Schultz, a trooper from Dunmore. Hacken wanted troopers who hadn't had any connection to the case in the past and who were responsible, tenacious investigators. The lieutenant told the two men to review all the evidence and then they'd meet to discuss it.

The troopers began their interviews in December 1994, talking to Ann Vitale and the Dillons.

In March of 1995, they called Bonnie Mead. At first, the secretary was wary. "Is this for real?" she asked testily.

She still wasn't sure she trusted that this investigation was really going somewhere. But things were starting to look promising.

Lieutenant Hacken asked the coroner, Robert Bartron, to petition the court to exhume the body of Martin Dillon. Bartron and his lawyer, Michael Giangrieco, had already met with Lieutenant Hacken and Dr. Isadore Mihalakis in Allentown to discuss what they could expect from a reautopsy. All agreed it had to be done.

On March 14, 1995, Bartron filed a petition for exhumation and reautopsy of Martin Thomas Dillon. In fighting the exhumation on Pat Scher's behalf, Peter O'Malley charged that the coroner was a close friend of the Dillons, and his request was thereby tainted. The lawyer put into the court record several letters Jo Dillon had written to her grandchildren over the years, in which she mentioned socializing with Bartron and his wife and occasionally keeping an eye on the funeral home for the couple when the Bartrons went snowmobiling in the Adirondack Mountains.

Six weeks later, a hearing was held at the Susquehanna County courthouse. Before Judge Kenneth Seamans, Dr. Isadore Mihalakis and Coroner Robert Bartron testified that an examination of the body of Martin Dillon was necessary to determine whether the initial finding of accidental death had been made in error. The two men told the judge that the initial autopsy had not been thorough. There were new questions about the manner of death; a reautopsy was critical to the search for answers.

On cross-examination, Peter O'Malley brought up the University of Pennsylvania medical examiners' conference in 1989. He asked Dr. Mihalakis if he was aware that DA Jeff Snyder had written a letter stating that most of the participants who examined the evidence believed the death of Martin Dillon had been an accident or suicide.

The courtroom spectators were stunned by Mihalakis's answer. The doctor flatly announced that he himself had attended that conference and the opposite was true—most of the pathologists and medical examiners believed the death was indicative of a homicide.

Clearly shaken, Peter O'Malley was unprepared for the doctor's response. He asked the judge for a continuance. Seamans promptly denied it.

"Call your first witness, Mr. O'Malley," Judge Seamans ordered.

The lawyer sighed. "You know I don't have a first witness, Judge," he said.

Judge Seamans rose from the bench. It was four-forty-five in the afternoon. "This court will hand down a decision before five P.M.," he said, walking out.

It did: The request for exhumation was granted.

CHAPTER 14

That night, Robert Bartron called the vault company and the gravediggers he'd already lined up and confirmed they would all meet the next morning at seven by the gate to Holy Name of Mary Cemetery. Worried that Peter O'Malley might appeal to the superior court to issue an injunction, Bartron was wasting no time.

On Saturday, April 29, 1995, the steel vault containing the casket of Martin Thomas Dillon was raised from the ground, loaded onto a truck, and taken to a secluded spot on Michael Giangrieco's property, where Robert Bartron cracked it open with a chisel. The mahogany casket was then hoisted out and placed in a hearse for the two-hour drive to Lehigh University Medical Center in Allentown.

In the autopsy room later that morning, Dr. Isadore Mihalakis opened the casket. Those on hand to witness the procedure were Lieutenant Hacken; Troopers

Stoud, Schultz and Schocin; Sergeant Weling; Coroner Bartron; Mihalakis's autopsy assistant Lysek, and a university student on a pathology rotation.

There was an eerie silence as each person stared at the near perfectly formed body of Martin Dillon.

It's almost viewable, Robert Bartron thought.

Indeed, interred in a dry, airtight seal, the body was in excellent condition.

Dr. Mihalakis removed the rosary beads still clasped in the hands and the wedding band inscribed *PRK to MTD 8/31/68*. The doctor handed the ring to Bartron for safekeeping.

For the next six hours, Dr. Mihalakis searched for answers. He measured the length of the arms and examined the type and size of the wound and its characteristics. He performed microscopic analysis of the skin at the impact area, looking for powder burns and gunpowder residue and their location on the body. By four o'clock Mihalakis was done, and the body was on its way back to Montrose.

All morning, as Peter O'Malley relaxed by his pool at home in Waverly, he'd been fighting an uneasy feeling. Finally, he gave up. He got dressed, thumbed through his files to find the name of the cemetery in Montrose, and drove half an hour north. He stopped in town and asked a passerby for directions to Holy Name of Mary Cemetery.

The attorney drove through the gate and began to circle the path. When he came to a pile of fresh dirt, he got out of his car, walked across the grass, and peered at the headstone next to a large cavity. *Martin Thomas Dillon.*

Peter O'Malley ran to his car and grabbed his cellular phone. He couldn't get a signal in the hills of

Montrose, so he sped down Route 11 until he got a stronger tone. He pulled over and called Dr. John Shane at home.

O'Malley told the doctor that the autopsy was taking place—at that very moment. "For God's sake," O'Malley practically shouted, "get over to that hospital as soon as you can."

It was a few hours before Dr. Shane called him back. "I've got some bad news for you," he said. "I got to the autopsy room and the place was clean as a whistle. No body, no nothing. I was looking for Mihalakis. I even tried to find his dinger."

"Dinger?" O'Malley asked.

"Yeah, they're the guys that clean up the slop," Shane said bluntly. "Mihalakis has his own dinger. Even he wasn't around."

In the weeks that followed, Dr. Isadore Mihalakis conducted a multitude of tests and experiments. He also examined other evidence—the microscopic trace of Dillon's blood on Scher's hunting boots, the cut stump stained with blood, the clothing of both Dillon and Scher, the broken 16-gauge shotgun, the spent magnum-load cartridge, the photographs of the body at the scene and at the original autopsy the following day. He reviewed Scher's statement to Collier, the report by Scales, and an earlier seventeen-page treatise by county detective Frank Bayer, indicating discrepancies in Scher's statement to Jock Collier. Mihalakis studied the FBI report on the blood spatter, indicating that the size of the droplets suggested that spatters were the by-product of high-velocity impact, and its pattern matched the shot in the 16-gauge shotgun. The doctor and state troopers experimented with a Winchester, identical in make and model to Scher's, that Michael Giangrieco had in his own gun collection. They attempted to simulate the angle of the entry wound by dropping the gun and exploring an array of possible angles and theories.

In May, Dr. Mihalakis submitted his thirteen-page report to the state police and Coroner Bartron. He found that the shot entered to the left of the sternum and went downward through the heart and left lung. The hole was oval and measured about one and a half inches in length and one inch in width. Pellets were found in the rear of Dillon's chest cavity.

Mihalakis determined that Martin Dillon could not have accidentally pulled the trigger if he had fallen over the 16-gauge shotgun. He would have hit the ground before the gun. There were no grass or dirt stains on his clothes or hands suggesting such a fall. It was also not possible that Dillon had snagged the weapon-trigger on a branch. Tests showed no gunpowder residue on the body, and the spread of pellet wounds suggested that the shot was fired from three to five feet away.

Mihalakis also concluded that investigators were unable to re-create dropping the weapon so that it discharged upon hitting the ground. The weight of the weapon would have caused the barrel to have pointed down had it been dropped.

In the end, Dr. Mihalakis found that evidence suggested Martin Dillon was crouched with his shirt billowing away from his chest when the magnum load passed right to left through his chest, destroying his heart. There were no burn marks on either clothing or skin, no marks a gun muzzle would have caused had the victim fallen on his weapon, no smoke deposits in the wound, and no blood on the gun barrel. The wound, Dr. Mihalakis found, also had scalloped edges, suggesting that the number 4 shot was beginning to spread from the plastic cartridge. That happens when the shotgun is at least several feet away.

If the gun barrel had been directly against Dillon's chest, in a fall or suicide, the shirt would have been taut. But the shirt he wore had a rent caused by the shotgun load that was offset from the wound. The clues ruled out a wound caused by the gun barrel being in contact with the body.

In his report, Dr. Mihalakis wrote:

> After review of the history and complete autopsy of the body of attorney Martin Dillon, death is attributed to a close range shotgun wound of the chest, not contact or near contact, and in this prosecutor's personal opinion it is to be beyond one foot and most likely even beyond two feet but less than six feet. Since at that range it is beyond self-infliction, the manner of death is homicide.

For a few weeks after receiving the report, Robert Bartron put off announcing its results aware of the reaction it would engender. As time passed, however, reporters began calling every day. Finally, on Tuesday morning, June 20, 1995, the coroner issued a terse press release.

> The Susquehanna County Coroner, Robert Bartron, has announced that the re-autopsy performed by Forensic Pathologist Dr. Isadore Mihalakis, from Allentown, has indicated in his

opinion that the cause of death of Attorney Martin T. Dillon who died on June 2, 1976, in Silver Lake Township, Susquehanna County, Pennsylvania, was a gunshot wound to the chest. Dr. Mihalakis indicated in his report that the specific manner of death of Attorney Martin T. Dillon was homicide.

The Susquehanna County coroner will have no further comment this time as the investigation is ongoing. Any further question can be directed to Lt. Francis Hacken of the Pennsylvania State Police.

At last, the wheels were in motion.

CHAPTER 15

Stephen Scher learned of the coroner's report in a phone call from Peter O'Malley, interrupting the doctor's workout at a Lincolnton gym. The attorney got right to the point. "Steve, I think you're about to be arrested."

"What should I do?" the doctor asked, starting to panic.

Not one to withhold dramatics, Peter O'Malley told him to get out of Lincolnton, fast.

"I'll tell you one thing I want to prevent," he said. "I don't want them picking you up in North Carolina and taking their good-natured time, staying overnight and throwing you into county jail. Who knows what will happen to your virginity along the way? You're not in good physical shape. People in prison do those things. I think you should come up here and surrender."

Stephen Scher didn't argue. He was petrified. "I've got to get my clothes," he said.

"Stay at the gym," O'Malley instructed. "Call your wife. She'll pack a suitcase for you. Just get here as fast as you can."

As soon as he hung up, Peter O'Malley began to make phone calls. If the Schers were coming to Pennsylvania, the press would surely like to know about it. He first called Chip Wilson, a reporter for the *Charlotte Observer* who'd been poking around Montrose in recent days. Wilson had stopped by O'Malley's Waverly home the evening before.

The reporter had been in touch with Susquehanna County officials, keeping up with the exhumation hearings from the *Observer*'s Gastonia bureau, not far from Lincolnton. After lobbying his editors for several weeks, Wilson finally received the go-ahead to pursue the story in Montrose. The day after he arrived, the coroner ruled the Dillon death a homicide. For Chip Wilson, the timing couldn't be better.

On the phone, O'Malley told the reporter that Stephen Scher was likely to be arrested but that he didn't want that to happen on North Carolina soil. He explained that the Schers were on their way to Pennsylvania; they might be available to the press the following day.

Chip Wilson was hopeful he'd have a chance to talk to the Schers. His interview with O'Malley the day before had gone fairly well—he found the lawyer frank and quotable. Chip had been surprised, however, at how stridently O'Malley attacked Larry Dillon, branding him "vicious" and "a bitter old man" for pursuing what he called a nineteen-year vendetta against his client.

On the day of Robert Bartron's announcement, Pat and Stephen Scher drove ten hours from Lincolnton to Waverly, arriving at their attorney's home after two in the morning. Stephen Scher walked through the front door with a heavy heart. The last time he'd been to Peter O'Malley's place had been three days after the shooting, when he'd tearfully related his story, convinced that Jock Collier would soon have him arrested. Collier was long gone, but Stephen Scher's fears seemed to be nearing reality.

O'Malley made coffee and the Schers stayed up for a few hours, talking.

"Steve, we all know they're going to arrest you," O'Malley told him bluntly. "They're not going to sleep until they do. It's a little dangerous, but let's accelerate the process. Let's call their bluff. Tell them to put up or shut up. Take the bull by the horns. Enough rumors and innuendo—if they have a case, they're going to arrest you. If they don't, they're not going to do anything. It's a crazy long shot. Most defense attorneys would never do anything like this. I lay it at your feet. You and Pat decide."

The Schers did. They took their attorney's advice.

"Let's call the press conference," Stephen Scher announced. "I want to tell my side of the story."

The next morning, O'Malley's secretary called the local television stations and newspapers, he had a sign made, "Press Conference," and ordered sodas and ice. The phone never stopped ringing. "Take a helicopter if you have to," O'Malley urged one reporter who called for directions.

When Chip Wilson arrived at O'Malley's home, Pat Scher, wearing jeans and a dungaree shirt, opened the front door. At first Chip thought the striking woman must be the daughter, Suzanne, but when she began complaining about how unfairly the press had been treating her family, he suddenly realized that this was the doctor's wife.

By midafternoon, about thirty reporters had gathered, mostly from the Binghamton, Scranton, and Wilkes-Barre areas. They set up cameras and microphones in O'Malley's living room.

The attorney opened the news conference dramatically. "This is probably the most unusual press conference you were ever at. I want to make a preliminary statement and I'll be finished. I'll turn Steve and Pat over to you. Enough is enough. State police, put up or shut up. You've harassed this man, you've harassed his family, neighbors. You told his daughter you'd buy her plane ticket if she'd come out and testify against him. She says, 'Keep your plane ticket. He's been my father ever since I was a little girl. I never heard him raise his voice, lose his temper. He never killed anybody.' Put up or shut up. Dr. Scher wants to be booked, fingerprinted, and mugged because he feels that he is innocent. . . . We are coming after them and they will pay dearly, all of them, including Dr. Mihalakis and his phony report."

Then it was Stephen Scher's turn. He cleared his throat and chose his words carefully. "I want to come forward, present myself to the state police and turn myself in and say, 'Arrest me and let's get on with this trial so I can forget about the last 19 years,' " he said firmly. "I did nothing to deserve this. I've been unfairly persecuted for the past 19 years. It's destroying my life . . . People don't look you in the eye and call you a murderer but they talk behind your back and your children hear it.''

A reporter asked him to explain what happened at Gunsmoke.

Scher repeated his original story. ''He saw a porcupine. He grabbed my gun and ran down the trail. I heard a click and then I heard the gunshot. I couldn't see him. I shouted something, I can't remember. I found him about three feet from the trail.''

Another journalist questioned Pat, wanting to know if she'd ever asked Stephen Scher if he was telling the truth about that day.

''I never had any reason to,'' Pat responded tersely. ''I have seen him carry dead patients to a stretcher, afraid that the undertaker would be too rough. I've seen him sit up with sick children. I know him as a kind and gentle giant. He is a healer. After Marty's death, everyone said to me, 'If you need any help, call us.' But he was the only one to help us. . . . My children have been irreparably damaged. It's been cruel and malicious and vicious and hateful. To think for even a second that something would happen where he would destroy a life—it's incomprehensible.''

Dr. Scher was asked point-blank if he killed Marty Dillon.

''Absolutely not,'' he said. ''Marty said, 'Wait here.' It was the last time I saw him alive. I heard nothing at first, then I heard a click and then I heard the shotgun.''

He told the reporters how he had tried to save Dillon. ''His face was ashen and blood was spurting from his chest,'' he said, his voice quivering. ''I knew it was hopeless, but I kept trying; he was my best friend."

O'Malley closed the press conference by facing the television cameras and announcing his home address so the state police knew where to find his client. He told the police Scher would be waiting for them.

The Pennsylvania state police were amused by O'Malley's tactic but had no intention of arresting their suspect just yet. They taped the press conference off the television news and jotted down various remarks Scher had made.

When reporters called the barracks for the department's response, Sergeant Raymond Hayes issued a brief statement. "Although we are very hopeful a successful prosecution will be initiated, it is doubtful that an arrest will be made in the immediate future. Loose ends have to be addressed. The burden of proof is on us. We cannot go forward on hearsay or innuendo."

Watching the television news that night, Ann Vitale was pleased that she had little reaction to seeing her former husband again. This is just a man I used to know, she thought.

She decided if he'd been able to destroy her, if she'd wound up living in squalor and working at McDonald's as he'd harshly predicted, she might feel differently. But Ann had a good life, a happy marriage, financial security. She felt no animosity toward Stephen Scher.

She marveled, though, at how she could still read him, even after all these years.

"I knew him for sixteen years, and he's just the same as he was," she told Bonnie Mead later. "The only giveaway that he was agitated or annoyed were particular gestures and phrases that he used that haven't changed. Yeah, they got to him. He's not as collected as he's making out to be.''

Once the press conference aired, Channel 16 in Scranton sent a camera crew to Lincolnton. A reporter went door to door, asking if neighbors knew that Dr. Stephen Scher was being investigated for a nineteen-year-old murder in Pennsylvania.

From that point on, the Schers' friends and parishioners from St. Dorothy's rallied around them.

Susan Burris and her husband, Ray, who ran a chiropractic office in town, had met the Schers at baseball games, track meets, and PTA meetings. The Burrises' son, John, was around the same age as Jonathan Scher. The couples quickly became good friends, and Susan Burris began to take her children to see Dr. Scher. Susan found him a giving man. She remembered how Dr. Scher had hurried from church to care for John when the boy burned himself on a friend's wood stove.

Susan Burris couldn't fathom the accusation coming out of Montrose. How can they even say that? she thought. How in the world can you say someone like him is capable of murder? He could never. He's in the business of saving lives, not taking them. I would bet my life. It's a family wrongly accused. His priorities are his patients.

Burris believed what Pat had told her in confidence as they'd become closer friends. She'd talked about her marriage to Marty and how his father never liked her and had been stirring up trouble ever since the shooting accident. Pat told Susan that Larry Dillon deeply resented her marriage to Stephen Scher. He couldn't accept it; he wouldn't leave them alone.

It's politics, Burris thought, when she heard the latest news from Pennsylvania. Things like that happen in families. They get mad, jealous.

Joan Mauldin thought so, too. A retired magistrate, the red-haired widow had been going to Dr. Scher as a patient ever since he'd opened his practice. When she heard of the allegations against the doctor, she told her son, Don, and daughter, Joyce, that it was absurd. Dr. Scher was a gentle man, a kind, compassionate physician. Mauldin had been to lots of doctors in the past who hadn't made her feel nearly as comfortable.

"I cannot imagine the person I know ever even being accused of something like that," she told her children. "Such a kind, gentle person, so dedicated in helping to heal and cure. I cannot believe he'd ever do anything to harm anybody. He acts like he has the time. He takes the time to listen to what problems you have."

The Reverend Farwell was the only one in Lincolnton who wasn't surprised by what was happening in Montrose. Once the fight over the exhumation ensued, the Schers had confided in Farwell about everything—detailing their version of the events at Gunsmoke and the Dillon family's malice toward Stephen Scher. Pat told the priest how Marty's parents never liked her, that they didn't care for Italians. The Schers maintained that after Marty's death they went in different directions, getting together much later.

The Reverend Farwell steadfastly believed in Stephen Scher's innocence. He tried to reassure the couple that the police investigation would go nowhere.

"It won't happen," he kept telling them. "It's

grasping at straws to reach the conclusion they're trying to reach. It's far-fetched.''

The Schers kept the priest updated about the hearings and called to let him know about the coroner's ruling. To The Reverend Farwell, the responsibility of this entire mess lay squarely on the shoulders of Larry and Jo Dillon. The elder Dillons, he felt, had simply never resolved their sorrow over the death of their son.

This is a reaction to their lack of grieving, this revenge and vendetta, the priest thought. Accidents do happen. Certainly you could draw colorful stories, but the people making these accusations have axes to grind.

The priest reassured Stephen Scher that God was with him. The Lord, Farwell told him, would hear his prayers.

CHAPTER 16

Within days of the coroner's announcement, District Attorney Jeffrey Snyder requested that the Pennsylvania attorney general's office appoint a special prosecutor to investigate the homicide. In a letter to Attorney General Thomas Corbett Jr., Snyder explained that his term in office was nearly over and he did not have the resources to prosecute the case, nor did Susquehanna County have the money to pay for it. The district attorney also maintained that he had acted professionally in his examination of the facts. "I feel that I have given all of the circumstances of this case the utmost consideration, and I have refused and resisted the temptation to act prematurely on the matter," he wrote.

Once the DA relinquished jurisdiction, Lieutenant Frank Hacken lobbied Corbett to get Robert Campolongo assigned to prosecute the case and was gratified when the attorney general agreed. A former

assistant district attorney in Philadelphia, Robert
Campolongo now worked in Norristown as senior
deputy attorney general. The fifty-six-year-old had
won more than 300 murder convictions in his career
and worked extensively with Lieutenant Hacken on
several of them. Brusque and rumpled in appearance,
Campolongo was a fierce and unyielding prosecutor
who had an erudite side—he was known to quote
Shakespeare and proffer obscure metaphors in arguments to the jury. Divorced with one grown son,
Campolongo was about to remarry Barbara Christie,
chief counsel to the Pennsylvania State Police. From
the moment he took on the prosecution of Stephen
Scher, he immersed himself in the case.

Meanwhile, the police investigation continued. Under Hacken's supervision, Troopers Schultz and
Stoud canvassed Susquehanna County and beyond,
interviewing dozens of witnesses. The troopers
hunted through payroll information to locate names
of staff members at Montrose General Hospital in the
early to mid-1970s and carefully checked off a list
Bonnie Mead culled of those who had information
about Dr. Stephen Scher's relationship with Marty
and Pat Dillon.

From the start, Hacken reminded his men that their
mission was to search for the truth, not to collect evidence to convict a suspect. It was a significant dis-
tinction for the lieutenant. Just thirty-four years old,
Frank Hacken had come to understand an important
credo of police investigations—the truth never
changes. Maintaining an unbiased approach to an investigation, he taught his staff, was crucial to law enforcement.

''In the beginning you don't have the total picture;

you don't know the importance of things upfront,"
he told them. "You have to analyze, you have to keep
an open mind. When you get tunnel vision, you may
disregard something. You must first understand before
you can be understood."

Early in their investigation, the troopers paid a visit
to Kendall Strawn. For the past ten years, Marty's
friend had been living on a 170-acre farm he'd purchased near Union Dale, about half an hour from
Montrose, raising Percheron draft horses and beef
cows. He was divorced now and lived with his girlfriend, Debbie Taylor, and two of her children. His
daughter, Tami, whose adoption had been arranged
by Stephen Scher and Pat Dillon, was twenty.

Kendall Strawn had heard in passing about at-
tempts to get an investigation into Marty's death
started, but he was still surprised finally to get a call
from the state police. He'd often thought about Marty
as the years passed. Once, in the mid-1980s, he'd received a phone call from Pat's brother, Robby Karveller, in Las Cruces, asking about the BMW he and
Marty bought a few years before Marty's death. Karveller explained that Michael Dillon was now competing in motorcycle tournaments and was interested
in his father's car.

Strawn confessed that the BMW was gone. He'd
loaned it to a professional race car driver who took it
to a competition a year or so after Marty died and
never returned it. When he told Karveller he hadn't
seen the car or the driver since then, Kendall Strawn
quickly sensed that Pat's brother did not believe him.

"That seems funny," Robby Karveller said, his
voice suddenly icy.

Strawn tried to convince Karveller he was telling the truth, but he gave up after a few minutes, and the conversation ended abruptly. The developer hung up the phone, disturbed. He'd done very well financially over the years, and he would have loved to have given the car to Marty's son as a gift. Kendall Strawn remembered Michael as a child, how Marty had been so proud of his boy.

Looking back, Strawn wished he'd tried to track down the car years ago. His life was so hectic at that time that he just never got around to looking into it. Kendall Strawn didn't blame Karveller for doubting his explanation—he knew it sounded a bit odd that he'd given up so easily on something as expensive as a car. But, Strawn reasoned, that's the way he was, and he couldn't change the past. If Karveller and Michael Dillon didn't believe him, there was nothing he could do about it.

In his meeting with the state police, Kendall Strawn struggled to recollect what he could about Marty, Pat, and Stephen Scher. He was fuzzy on dates—he couldn't recall how often he'd cautioned Marty about Pat's friendship with Dr. Scher, or exactly when he and Marty went to Florida for a race and Dr. Scher was coming to the Dillons' to put Pat in traction. He did, however, clearly remember the undertones back then, and the mood. He could still see Pat's face when he asked about her back problem as he and Marty were leaving, how nervously she'd answered, how obviously she was lying.

And Kendall Strawn had no trouble recounting in detail the night in the Dillons' basement at 7 Kelly Street, at Marty's thirtieth birthday party. Twenty years later, Strawn could still picture Stephen Scher's face as Marty toasted the gathering, the utter malice in the doctor's glare.

The troopers asked if he'd be willing to testify to that, and Kendall Strawn didn't hesitate.

"I'll be there," he told them. "Just tell me when."

Strawn wasn't able to help the state police when they asked about the 12-gauge double-barreled Ithaca shotgun Marty had been using the day he died. It had been Strawn's shotgun—he'd loaned it to Marty after the lawyer said he'd been thinking of buying one. Strawn vaguely recalled getting it back a few months after Marty's death. The state police had given it to Marty's dad, and Larry Dillon had called him to pick it up.

Kendall searched his gun collection and hunted through the attic and the barn. He even called his ex-wife and his eighty-four-year-old father to see if they remembered anything about it. He felt sheepish admitting he couldn't find it, but the troopers told him not to worry—it wasn't a pivotal piece of evidence.

The investigators met one by one with the doctors, nurses, and receptionists from Montrose General. They interviewed Rosalie Richards and Betty Williams and heard their nearly identical stories of walking in on Scher and Pat Dillon kissing and touching in the drug room. They listened to Sandra Jean Price as she related seeing Stephen Scher squeeze Pat Dillon's breasts in a hospital corridor, and Elaine Henninger, who disclosed the couple's penchant for going into room 13. They spoke with Dr. Bertsch and Dr. Bennett, both still practicing at Montrose General, and tracked down the former receptionist, Jo Ann Warner, now a married high school teacher and mother of two

sons, who told them about all the times Scher gave
Pat Dillon's phone number when he was on call.

They talked to neighbors including Nancy Frey,
who had lived next door to Pat and Marty, who told
of seeing Scher at the house all the time, and Elaine
Henninger, who lived on Ridge Road and watched as
Scher's car passed by practically every day. They interviewed Judith Vaccaro, who lived across the street
from 7 Kelly Street and had seen Scher and Pat kissing in the driveway, and Judge Donald O'Malley,
who had recused himself from hearing the Schers'
divorce because he, too, frequently saw the doctor's
car in the Dillon driveway. Investigators found the
former paperboy, Dan Calby, who described waiting
on the porch steps before a frazzled Pat Dillon hurried
to the door.

The troopers spoke to those who'd been to Gunsmoke on June 2—Susan and Don Strope, the game
protectors, and the state police. They interviewed Ed
Little three times. The chagrined former district attorney confessed that he now realized he'd made a
mistake, that if he had it to do over again he would
have investigated the shooting. He tried to explain
how he'd rationalized that it had been an accident. "I
didn't think a respectable doctor would do this when
he was the only person there, nor add fuel to the fire
by marrying the widow of the victim," he said.
"That's how I analyzed it in my mind."

Little also conceded that he couldn't remember
many details from the past. When the investigators
asked him whether he'd coauthored a letter with Jock
Collier to the county commissioners, suggesting that
the case be investigated further, Little said he didn't
know. "If it comes down to what other people say

and what I say, believe the other people,'' he told the troopers.

In the fall of 1995, the state police went to Las Cruces and interviewed Pat's mother, Laura Karveller, who quickly blamed the Dillons for this vendetta against her son-in-law. She told them that Larry and Jo Dillon never liked her daughter and snubbed her and her husband at the wedding because the Karvellers were foreigners. She said that at the graveside, she heard Larry Dillon vow revenge for his son's death and that at the lunch following the burial the Dillons forced the Karvellers to move from the family table.

But Laura Karveller told the investigators something else—that she was in her daughter's living room the night of June 2 and heard Dr. Scher's explanation of what happened, how he and Marty had been inside the trailer and Marty had jumped up, grabbed a shotgun by the door, and run out.

Laura Karveller didn't know it, but Stephen Scher gave a markedly different version of the events of June 2 to Trooper Hairston and Jock Collier. Unwittingly, Pat's mother helped cast further doubt on her son-in-law's story.

Of all the information culled, the state police were particularly fascinated with what they uncovered at the home of Tom and Carol Gazda. Trooper Jamie Schultz had been assigned to talk to Tom Gazda, as one of the first EMTs at the scene. Schultz had finished taking a statement from Gazda and was getting ready to leave when Carol Gazda, who'd been listening silently, said she had something to add.

She disclosed that she, too, had been to Gunsmoke, that she'd waited in the car with her young daughter after her husband had waved them away from the scene. Carol Gazda then described the man she'd seen, crying as soon as anyone appeared, relaxed and dry-eyed when he was alone.

Jamie Schultz was astonished. He hadn't known Carol Gazda was even at Gunsmoke. He instantly recognized that what she was telling him revealed a great deal about the suspect.

Carol Gazda explained that at the time, she didn't know what had occurred at the camp or who any of the people there were. She told Schultz that because they lived just a few miles from the New York state line they went across the border to shop and to go to doctors. They didn't know anyone from Montrose.

It was later that night, when her husband returned after eleven, that Carol said she learned of the shooting. She was lying in bed when her husband walked into the room and told her there had been an accident, that a man had tripped and fallen on his gun and had been killed instantly. As Jamie Schultz continued to write feverishly, Carol Gazda reported her reaction, almost two decades earlier, to her husband's words.

"I said, 'I bet it's murder. That was no accident,'" Gazda declared.

Jamie Schultz could hardly wait to share the latest interview with his partner, Steve Stoud, and Lieutenant Hacken. He thought about his supervisor's maxim about gathering everything until the picture becomes clear. This was a small piece, he knew, but it might well turn out to be an important part of the puzzle.

As the investigation progressed, the Schers girded for a fight to have another autopsy performed on the body of Martin Dillon, this time by their own experts. They retained the foremost forensic pathologists in the country—Dr. Cyril Wecht and Dr. Michael Baden— at $3,500 a day, and in addition to Peter O'Malley hired Richard Sprague, a high-priced Philadelphia attorney. After the coroner's declaration of homicide, Sprague immediately filed a request for reautopsy, listing Pat Scher and her children, Michael and Suzanne Dillon, as the petitioners. The three charged that a third autopsy was necessary to dispel the insinuation that Stephen Scher was responsible for Martin Dillon's death. The petition alleged that the livelihood of Pat Dillon and her children were threatened by the accusation against the doctor.

> *The press speculation of Stephen Scher's involvement in the death of Martin Dillon has caused great personal anguish and emotional distress to Patricia Dillon Scher and her children . . . In addition, Applicant's future income, which is tied to that of her husband, will be placed in jeopardy if an immediate re-autopsy for her benefit and protection is not granted.*

In the suit, Sprague also demanded that Coroner Robert Bartron release a copy of Isadore Mihalakis's report, but Bartron's lawyer, Michael Giangrieco, advised the coroner to refuse. In motions to the court, Senior Deputy Attorney General Robert Campolongo contended that the Schers had no right to the information because a criminal investigation was ongoing, and Stephen Scher had not yet been charged with anything.

Campolongo's brief urged the judge to dismiss the petition, labeling it spurious and without standing: "Nowhere in the petition does Patricia Scher deny that the death of her husband was a homicide. Nowhere does she deny that her current husband is the perpetrator. Nowhere does she even allude to the fact with hands free of guilt.''

Campolongo pointed out that Patricia Scher failed to appear at hearings for the prior petitions and didn't appeal the original April 28, 1995, exhumation order. Campolongo told the judge that the exhumation had not been a secret—it was recorded and reported by the press as early as eleven Saturday morning. He charged in court that the physician retained by the Schers, Dr. John Shane, didn't appear at the hospital until after the autopsy was completed. The prosecutor added that even then Peter O'Malley never sought a special injunction to keep the body in Allentown.

At a hearing before Judge Kenneth Seamans at the Susquehanna County Court of Common Pleas, Michael Dillon, now twenty-four years old, flew in from Las Cruces and testified that he, his sister, and his mother wanted a pathologist of their own to review the coroner's conclusion that his father's death had been a homicide. The young man made it clear that he was steadfast in his support of his stepfather. ''I know Stephen Scher had nothing to do with my father's death,'' he told the court.

Michael Dillon went on to say that his mother was a very caring person and the press attention was devastating to her. ''With headlines like this and people calling and state troopers casing the house she is becoming withdrawn,'' he explained to the judge. ''She looks ill, tired and cannot concentrate on her job, on her livelihood. I understand that the Coroner of the county believes that it was a homicide and I would like my own experts to look into this and tell me what they think. I think I have a right to know that because Martin Dillon is my father. Dr. Scher is the man that raised me. I'm not sure how else I can explain that.''

Despite Michael Dillon's emotional appeal, Judge Kenneth Seamans was not convinced. He ruled that Pat Scher had not proved that her future income would be jeopardized if a third autopsy was not performed. As for the children, Seamans wrote in his decision that their claims were unfounded. ''Michael and Suzanne Dillon have made no showing that an exhumation and autopsy are imperatively required beyond the fact that they are upset by the speculation engendered by the coroner's declaration to the press that Martin Dillon's death was a homicide. They have shown no injury to themselves or to their mother which a re-exhumation and reautopsy would rectify. Moreover they have in no way shown that an autopsy conducted by pathologists of their choosing would resolve once and for all the truth regarding the death of Martin Dillon.''

Peter O'Malley spoke to reporters on the steps of the courthouse minutes after the decision was handed down. ''I say this respectfully,'' he announced. ''The last say is not in this courthouse.''

He was right. It took almost a year and cost the Schers some $400,000 in legal fees, but in the spring of 1996 a superior court overturned Judge Seamans's ruling and permitted the exhumation of the body of Martin Dillon for the second time. The court also ordered that Coroner Robert Bartron turn over Dr. Mihalakis's autopsy report.

It was May 11, 1996, when O'Malley and his team of gravediggers arrived at Holy Name of Mary Cemetery in a cold, driving rain. The attorney waited, shivering, in his car. Suddenly, the door was yanked open.

Standing in the rain was an angry Jo Dillon. "What are you doing?" she demanded.

"Who are you?" O'Malley asked.

"You know who I am," she retorted. "I'm Marty Dillon's mother."

Peter O'Malley was annoyed. "Don't ever yank a door open on me like that again," he snapped. "You know darn well what we're doing and we have a court order that allows us to do it. I don't have to show it to you but I'd be happy to as a matter of courtesy."

Jo Dillon wasn't interested in court orders. She was incensed. "How dare you do this on his birthday," she said harshly.

Peter O'Malley was taken aback. He noticed the flowers in Jo Dillon's hands. "Well, I didn't know it was his birthday," O'Malley said a bit more chagrined, "and I'm sorry. But what has to be done, has to be done. You had your autopsy, we're entitled to ours."

Later that day, the Schers finally got what they wanted—their own expert, Dr. John Shane, performed a third autopsy on the body of Martin Dillon. When it was completed, the body was returned to Holy Name of Mary Cemetery. But it wasn't interred beneath the tombstone that bore Martin Dillon's name.

At Pat Scher's insistence and with the support of her children, the casket was lowered into the ground in an unmarked grave about thirty yards away from the original site, in an area where the Karveller family owned a small plot. It was a strikingly bitter declaration.

When Bonnie Mead heard the latest salvo from Pat Scher and her children, she dissolved into tears. Larry and Jo Dillon, however, did not. Jo Dillon even called Bonnie at work to comfort her.

"It's only his body, Bonnie. His soul is with the Lord," the older woman reminded her gently. "Pat is looking for a fight, and we're not going to give it to her."

Indeed, by this time, the Dillons at last trusted that their patience would soon be rewarded. It was. The very next month, Lieutenant Frank Hacken and Senior Deputy Attorney General Robert Campolongo reviewed the evidence and agreed that they were ready. Troopers Schultz and Stoud prepared an eight-page affidavit of probable cause, outlining the commonwealth's case against the doctor. Once it was signed by the two troopers as well as Judge Seamans, a copy was faxed to the North Carolina State Bureau of Investigation. A task force was assembled of state bureau officers to pick up the suspect.

On June 20, 1996, exactly twenty years and eighteen days after a shotgun blast split the quiet at Gunsmoke, Troopers Stoud and Schultz and Special Agent Ted Bugda got into a van and headed to Lincolnton, North Carolina.

It was time to bring Dr. Stephen Scher back.

CHAPTER 17

The arrest of Dr. Stephen Scher for murder shook the town of Lincolnton.

It was late morning when the team of agents in unmarked cars pulled into the parking lot of the allergy office on Dave Warlick Drive. Next door, at Davis' auto body shop, owner Randy Davis put down his tools and watched in amazement as plainclothes officers, guns drawn, surrounded the office and several proceeded inside. Minutes later, almost a dozen patients hurried out, some in tears. Then, Dr. Stephen Scher appeared in handcuffs, was placed in the backseat of a car, and driven off. A stunned and sobbing Pat Scher remained in the office with the staff.

Randy Davis immediately called Lincoln County Sheriff Barbara Pickens and told her what he'd just witnessed. The sheriff was taken aback. She was aware of the investigation—a year earlier Pennsylvania state troopers had met with her to discuss the allegations against Scher, and she'd recently heard from a local attorney that an indictment was expected to be handed down in Susquehanna County.

But Pickens had heard nothing from law enforcement officials regarding an arrest. Although the State Bureau of Investigation had original jurisdiction over the case, her department had assisting jurisdiction. Always in the past, there'd been good cooperation between the Lincoln County office and other law enforcement organizations.

Not this time, however. Sheriff Pickens didn't like what she was hearing from Randy Davis.

"There were patients in there," he told her. "There were guys outside with guns. What's going on?"

"I have no earthly idea," she replied. "I hadn't heard a thing about it. Were there any city police with them?"

Davis told her he hadn't seen any.

Pickens called the city police at once and confirmed that they, too, knew nothing about an arrest. Almost immediately, Pickens's administrative assistant began fielding calls from reporters. Minutes after the doctor had been apprehended, the office of the Pennsylvania state attorney general faxed a press release to a host of media outlets, announcing the arrest and including a copy of the affidavit of probable cause.

Sheriff Pickens didn't know what to tell the reporters. Since she'd taken over the eighty-one-member department in 1994 as the first elected female sheriff in North Carolina, she'd maintained a good relationship with the press—they respected her, and she, them. She'd understood the politics of dealing with the media from her ten years as chief deputy.

Pickens picked up the phone and called Jim Woodward, the sergeant in charge at the State Bureau of Investigation in Huntersville, whom she'd known for more than twenty-five years. Struggling to contain her anger, Pickens told him she had no problem with an outside agency handling an arrest but she thought it was extremely bad form not to notify the sheriff and the chief of police.

"We didn't know who these people were," she said. "What if somebody over there pulled a gun? What if a citizen didn't know they were officers? We could have had a real bad situation on our hands. We couldn't answer reporters' questions. We try to be very cooperative with the media. You put us in a bad position."

Woodward didn't offer an apology, but Pickens wasn't looking for one. She wanted her displeasure known, and it was.

Following the arrest, Stephen Scher was taken to the local court where arrest papers were processed, and then he was escorted to the Lincoln County jail. Pickens's chief deputy, Bill Beam, met him there. When Beam arrived, a member of the task force started to inform him of the afternoon plans for the suspect, but Beam set him straight in a hurry. "Any inmate is turned over to us, they are in our custody," he said firmly. "That's the law. We run the jail. Once you deliver him to us, you're done."

"We have to take him back to court," the officers told him.

"I understand that," Beam shot back. "But *we'll* deliver him."

Bill Beam could tell that the jail staff felt intimidated by the FBI agents, but he did not. He also knew that the agents recognized that he now was in the position of authority, and Beam wasn't going to let them forget it. He told them what he thought about the way they'd handled the arrest of Dr. Stephen Scher.

"We knew these charges," he said sternly. "As far as a security risk, there was none with this man. We didn't have any knowledge of this before. We should have been told."

When reporter Chip Wilson heard the news of the arrest, he made the twenty-minute trip from the *Charlotte Observer*'s Gastonia bureau to Lincolnton in under ten. All the while, he hoped he wasn't too late for the bond hearing. When he arrived at the courthouse, he learned that Dr. Scher was in custody at the Lincoln County Jail and officers said there would be no court appearance that day.

Wilson was suspicious and decided to wait. His hunch paid off. By three o'clock, shortly after several reporters who'd gathered at the courthouse had left, the judge called a hearing to order, and Dr. Stephen Scher appeared beside a local attorney he'd recently retained. In a short proceeding, the court upheld the legality of the fugitive warrant and agreed with Lincoln County prosecutor Mike Randall that the seriousness of the charge meant there was no obligation to grant the defendant bond.

Stephen Scher opted to fight extradition to Pennsylvania. Given his behavior at Peter O'Malley's press conference a year earlier, when he and his lawyer all but dared authorities to arrest him, it seemed especially telling. It confirmed what was already obvious to Robert Campolongo and the prosecution team he'd put in place: Stephen Scher's demand for a trial to clear his name was spurious. Indeed, the last thing Stephen Scher wanted was to relate his account of what happened at Gunsmoke to a jury.

Larry and Jo Dillon learned of the arrest from Frank Hacken. The lieutenant had called the couple earlier that morning at Gunsmoke and said he planned to drop by. When he arrived he asked to use the phone, and the Dillons waited as Hacken listened and spoke quietly into the receiver for several minutes. When he hung up, the lieutenant turned to the couple and said simply, ''They have just arrested Dr. Scher.''

The Dillons embraced, immensely relieved and gratified. As they thanked the lieutenant for all his hard work, Frank Hacken reminded them that the future was uncertain. ''There's a long, hard road to go,'' he said.

Marty's parents understood. With God to guide them, they said, they could endure whatever unfolded.

Peter O'Malley wasn't just stunned to learn of Stephen Scher's arrest, he was furious. The lawyer was convinced that the state police timed the arrest so that he would be unavailable to his client.

Earlier that month, O'Malley had been hospitalized briefly in Scranton for phlebitis, and against his physician's advice he had flown to Colorado Springs to visit his thirty-three-year-old son, Peter, Junior. The altitude, his doctor had warned, could cause complications. But O'Malley had been feeling better and was looking forward to a few weeks hiking in the mountains.

The attorney realized within hours of his arrival that he'd made a mistake. The higher elevation made him feel disoriented and woozy, and he began to slur his speech and repeat himself. Concerned, O'Malley's son rushed him to the hospital, where doctors discovered that the lawyer's lungs were filled with water. Fearing blood clots due to his history of phlebitis, Peter O'Malley was admitted and told he could not be moved. When he heard of his client's arrest, there was little the attorney could do.

Stephen Scher ultimately decided not to fight extradition to Pennsylvania and on Monday, June 24, 1996, he was placed in shackles for the five-hundred-mile trip to Montrose. Special Agent Ted Bugda drove almost the entire way.

The ten-hour trip ended at the state police barracks in Dunmore where Stephen Scher was fingerprinted and photographed. He was then transported to the district justice's tiny courtroom in Harford, not far from Montrose. By now, it was almost nine o'clock.

In leg irons and handcuffs, clutching a copy of *The New American Bible*, Dr. Stephen Scher was arraigned on charges that he murdered Martin Dillon on June 2, 1976.

Alice Collier was eighty-two years old, her health slowly deteriorating from kidney failure, when the news broke that Dr. Stephen Scher had been charged with the murder of Martin Dillon. Her granddaughter, Christina Fisher, brought her the front-page stories in the *Binghamton Press & Sun Bulletin* and in the local *Susquehanna Transcript* and read them aloud. Alice Collier hugged and kissed her granddaughter.

"He was right all along," she said, beaming. "I just wish Jock was alive to see this."

She called her son Kenny. "Why didn't they listen to Jock twenty years ago?" she asked him.

In the two decades since the death of Marty Dillon, it hadn't been only the young lawyer's friends and family who grieved; Alice Collier had mourned as well. She'd felt her husband's pain when he'd come through the door after a long talk with Larry Dillon and in his weeks of silence during the holiday season. At night, she sensed the tension in Jock's body as he lay next to her, his mind racing. Even after Jock's death, Alice Collier often said a prayer for the couple she'd never met, the family whose lives had such a profound effect on her husband.

After Scher's arrest, Alice Collier was saddened to hear that the Dillon children wanted nothing to do with their grandparents.

"Those poor people," she told Kenny. "They didn't only lose a son, they lost grandchildren, too. Those children didn't even know their own father. Now they won't know their grandparents, either."

Five months after the arrest, Alice Collier died in her son's home. Weeks earlier, she'd told him how grateful she was that she'd lived to see Jock's goal accomplished.

Jock's friends felt the same way. Dick Pelicci, the Susquehanna County sheriff, decided Jock must be around, somewhere in Montrose. The somber county detective couldn't miss this.

He's here, Pelicci often thought, surveying the night sky. He knows it happened.

CHAPTER 18

Within days of her husband's arrest, Pat Scher phoned various friends and family members and asked an important favor—that they come to Montrose on June 27 and testify at a bail hearing about Stephen Scher's character and reputation. One by one, everyone she called agreed immediately.

Joan Mauldin, Scher's patient, wasn't surprised by Pat's request. As a retired magistrate, Mauldin had been asked to be a character witness many times in the past.

"If there's anything I can do, I will," she told Pat. "I do not mind saying what I know. I know nothing but good."

The Reverend Farwell didn't hesitate to help, either. He'd been on vacation at the beach in Wilmington, North Carolina, when Pat called with the news of the arrest. Farwell flew to Scranton and stayed with Pat's cousin prior to the hearing.

By now, Peter O'Malley had returned to Pennsylvania from Colorado but was still too ill to appear in court. His brother Todd, also a lawyer, agreed to stand in for him.

From home, Peter O'Malley dictated a brief arguing for bail. In it, O'Malley pointed out that Scher was married and lived with his wife and their fifteen-year-old son, Jonathan. He told the court that Stephen Scher was active in civic and community affairs and regularly attended St. Dorothy's Catholic Church. He added that the doctor was in questionable health, having undergone open heart surgery, and that Scher had high blood pressure and was experiencing cardio-vascular problems. O'Malley pointed out that a year earlier Scher had offered to surrender within one hour of learning about the coroner's report, and again, as recently as May 1996, he had offered to turn himself in upon notice that an arrest was forthcoming. The brief stressed that Stephen Scher needed to be released so that he could continue to practice medicine to support his family and to contest the charges he faced.

The large courtroom on the second floor of the Susquehanna County Court of Common Pleas quickly filled on the morning of June 27. Supporters of the Dillon family gathered on the right side; friends of Stephen Scher sat on the left.

Kendall Strawn showed up, and so did Bonnie Mead. Larry and Jo Dillon, however, remained at Gunsmoke. The prosecution team, wary that the couple could be called by the defense to testify, requested that they stay away. Jo's cousin, Bill Nash, and his wife, Vonda, went in their place and promised to call as soon as they had news.

Following O'Malley's advice, Pat Scher did not attend the hearing. But Suzanne Dillon, now twenty-two and working as a costume designer, flew in from Colorado Springs to be there for her stepfather. Medium height and slim, she wore a black suit, her hair dyed auburn and cropped short. She stood next to a row of her family's supporters, her eyes scanning the crowded courtroom.

Just before the hearing began, Kendall Strawn approached her. "Suzanne, I'm Ken Strawn," he said.

The strapping developer towered over the young woman, but Suzanne Dillon was clearly not fazed. She knew who he was—she'd heard his name from her mother. She looked him directly in the eye. "Whose side are you sitting on?" she asked abruptly.

Kendall Strawn looked sad. "Suzanne," he said gently, "I'm not here to take sides." He smiled at her. "You look just like your dad."

"I'm very proud of that," she responded a bit sharply.

Kendall nodded. "I know it's hard for you."

Suzanne didn't answer, but her expression softened. Then the bailiff called the court to order.

Seconds later, Dr. Stephen Scher was led into the courtroom in handcuffs. His eyes immediately went to his stepdaughter, and Suzanne smiled and nodded encouragingly, her eyes instantly filling with tears. She mouthed, "I love you." Stephen Scher smiled.

Throughout the morning, Todd O'Malley called witnesses to testify to Scher's good character and reliability.

"He's known to be a compassionate doctor," The

Reverend Farwell told the court. "I've been in their home many times and I've found them to be a loving and close family. Dr. Scher supports the church financially. Pat teaches in Sunday School. The children attend Sunday School."

On cross-examination, Robert Campolongo asked the priest several times about donations Scher made to the church, implying that was the reason Farwell spoke so well of him. Then the senior deputy attorney general turned his attention to another matter. Since the defense called a Catholic priest to the stand, Robert Campolongo intended to make use of him.

"The Catholic Church does not believe in divorce, is that correct?" he asked.

The priest hesitated. "I'm not sure how to answer."

Campolongo tried again. "In 1976 did the Catholic Church believe in divorce?"

"It's a sacramental bond that cannot be broken," Farwell explained. "Divorce is a civil term."

Campolongo ignored him. "I'm talking about two Catholics who go to church—Patricia Dillon, Martin Dillon, get married in church," he said flatly. "The Catholic Church would not permit divorce."

Before Farwell could answer, Todd O'Malley objected. "It's way beyond the scope," he complained.

The judge agreed, and Campolongo shrugged. He'd made his point.

Joan Mauldin testified next. She said she'd known Dr. Scher ever since he moved to Lincolnton four years earlier.

"He's a very good doctor," she told the court. "I've been in his home, he's been in mine. He loves his family."

"What is his relationship with his patients?" Todd O'Malley asked. "Would he walk out on them?"

She said he wouldn't.

On cross-examination, Campolongo jumped to his feet. "Any idea of what his reputation may have been in Pennsylvania when he resided here?" he barked.

"No sir, I don't."

"Did you know of his reputation as a philanderer?" Before Mauldin could answer, Campolongo continued. "All you know is what you've observed in the last four years."

Mauldin had to agree.

Mary Jane Neikirk, Scher's bookkeeper, testified about the doctor's practice, telling the court that he grossed about $350,000 a year. Carl Keuhner, whose wife was Pat's first cousin, spoke of Dr. Scher's devotion to his family. "Dr. Scher took over the education and support of both Suzanne and Michael Dillon," he said. "Along the way they adopted Jonathan. He has provided lovingly for all three children to this day."

Dr. Daniel Allan testified that since he moved to Las Cruces in 1981, four years after Dr. Scher, the two had become close friends. Allan told the court that in the last six months he loaned Scher $30,000 and paid for Suzanne Dillon's airline ticket to Pennsylvania.

"His relationship with his patients is outstanding," Allan testified. "They love him."

Wendall Miller, the director of medical staff development for Lincolnton Medical Center, called himself a friend as well as a business associate of Scher. He testified that the doctor accepted Medicaid and Medicare patients.

Pat Scher's good friend from Las Cruces, Susie Drumm, now divorced and using the last name Horton, took the stand and said that she'd traveled from New Mexico to testify on behalf of Dr. Stephen Scher. She told the court how she had met the Schers in 1978 when her former husband owned a jewelry store and they became close friends of the couple. She said everyone in Las Cruces spoke highly of Dr. Scher.

"He was probably one of the most loved physicians," she said. "He would do anything for his patients."

The highlight of testimony was at the end, when Suzanne Dillon testified. The young woman, clearly a bit nervous, told the judge of the wonderful life she'd had as the daughter of Stephen Scher.

"He's been a fantastic father, textbook," she said, her voice shaking slightly. "He's been financially supportive, emotionally supportive. He's been the most stable thing in my life. He treats his patients with compassion. He's an excellent doctor. They love him. . . . He's the only dad I've ever known. . . . My Dad's great."

She insisted that Stephen Scher was not a bail risk. "He wouldn't leave because he can't leave. He is first and foremost a doctor. He's a responsible physician. He can't leave."

In response to a question from Todd O'Malley about the family's finances, Suzanne's animosity was evident as she related what the charges against her stepfather had done to her family.

"It's ruined us," she announced. "We're broke. We have nothing. It's all gone. The only way he can make any money is what he can make tomorrow until he dies.''

Suzanne Dillon then stunned the courtroom with her next declaration: She'd turned over the money she received from her father's life insurance policy to Stephen Scher to help pay legal costs. Suzanne testified that her share of the insurance money, invested since 1976, totaled $65,000. She added that she never wavered in her desire to help in any way she could. Her reason was clear. ''Because he's my Dad,'' she told the court. ''That's what you do when you're family.''

When the witnesses had finished testifying, Todd O'Malley addressed the judge. In his argument to release Stephen Scher without bail or with a reasonable amount, O'Malley stressed the doctor's devotion to his patients and his family. He reminded the judge that Scher had strong ties to his community and to his church.

In his argument against bail, Robert Campolongo attacked the witnesses brought by O'Malley, arguing that the defendant had simply manipulated them and that none of them knew him when he lived in Pennsylvania in 1976.

''He's got the wheels turning all the time,'' the prosecutor told Seamans. ''He even has his own stepchild, the child of the deceased, testifying for him. What does she know about this? I don't believe the sob story told by the daughter—he would never flee, he wouldn't leave his patients. He was out of town pretty quick in 1976.''

Campolongo stressed the seriousness of the charges, that the evidence against Scher was strong. He told the court that the defendant was at great risk for flight. ''He has severed his ties here,'' he told the court. "He's looking at life in prison. The defendant may not want to pay the piper."

Judge Kenneth Seamans sided with the prosecution. After a brief recess, he handed down his ruling. "After consideration of the matters testified to in the bail hearing and evidence taken, in addition to consideration of the brief presented by defense counsel, this court being of the opinion that the nature of the crime charged is serious and in addition to that, that the ties of the defendant to the Commonwealth of Pennsylvania are minimal, bail is hereby set at the sum of one million dollars."

It was a major victory for the prosecution. Supporters of Stephen Scher sat stonily, stunned by the judge's decision. To make matters worse, the judge ruled that if Scher chose to put up real estate as bail, only property from the Commonwealth of Pennsylvania could be used.

The courtroom began to empty. Kendall Strawn couldn't resist confronting the man he believed killed his best friend. He walked to the front of the courtroom where Scher was seated at the defense table, and stage-whispered, "Steve, was it worth it?"

Stephen Scher did not turn around. Kendall Strawn, satisfied, started to walk away.

Suddenly, a red-faced Suzanne Dillon was pushing through the crowd, pursuing Strawn. "Excuse me, sir," she called out to him, her voice loud and angry. "What did you say to my father?"

Strawn turned and faced the young woman. His face, too, was red with emotion. "Suzanne, you were too young to know," he told her frankly.

"What did you say to my father?" Suzanne repeated.

"You were too young to understand then and you're too young now."

Suzanne just stared at him. "And you're too ignorant," she snapped and turned away.

Outside the courthouse, Scher's friends expressed disbelief at the bail set by the judge.

Susie Horton told reporters that Scher had been wrongly accused. "If Pat had questions, if anything was askew, she wouldn't have married him. It's almost evil what's going on here. It's so blatantly one-sided."

Joan Mauldin thought so, too. She told reporters that the bail hearing had been completely unfair. "I've never seen anything like this," she said. "It's something right out of a movie. It seems to me the town had made their minds up. I feel a lot of animosity here. I know nothing about Pennsylvania law but that wasn't the way we would have done it. It was a farce. Everything had been decided upon. I can see how the DA could ask for that but I don't know what the judge was thinking to allow it. Pennsylvania law may be entirely different but I thought the purpose of bond was universal. How totally ridiculous, how vindictive. If the man was going to run, he would have been gone. Bail is not to punish, it's to assure their appearance in court. If he wasn't going to appear, he would have gone to Timbuktu a long time ago."

She went on to say that she couldn't imagine that the prosecution had a case anyway. "I can't know what went on 20 years ago, all I know is what I know in my heart. Whatever they have now they had then. Surely to goodness, if something was wrong why didn't they do it 20 years ago? I don't know how this is possible. A lot of witnesses passed on. How in the world do they think they'll get a conviction?''

She said she was more determined than ever to do whatever she could to help the Schers. "I would do anything I could to help this man and this lady. It looks to me like they really are in for unpleasant times if this thing is tried there. He's not the bear they try to make him out to be.... Suzanne is a fine young lady and she loves Dr. Scher with all her heart. She supports him 100 percent. This man could not be bad and have a young person such as she willing to say the things she did. It only reaffirms my belief that he is a good man.''

After the hearing, Reverend Farwell spent time with Pat and Suzanne and some of Pat's relatives. He told them he had been to many trials and custody hearings in his twenty-five years of service, but he'd never seen anything like what he'd just witnessed in Montrose.

"I don't know what law they're practicing in Pennsylvania," he told them. "One million dollars bail? It was a setup.''

He expressed his bitterness about the references to Scher's donations to the church. "I resent that. I'm surprised at the viciousness and hatred generated.''

Having done all he could, The Reverend Farwell headed back to Lincolnton. It's a bizarre comedy of tragic consequences, he thought. It doesn't fit with the man I know, and I've been around some pretty evil people. It's like a Shakespeare comedy and tragedy all wrapped up. He's a man of integrity, a good man.

Clearly the Commonwealth of Pennsylvania did not agree. When Peter O'Malley learned about the one-million-dollar bond the lawyer realized he needed help. He asked his brother Todd to call John Moses, a well-connected Wilkes-Barre attorney with a strong foundation in law and extensive experience with appeals.

"He's almost as good as I am," O'Malley later explained to a reporter.

CHAPTER 19

When John Moses's secretary informed him that he had a call from a Scranton attorney named Todd O'Malley, he assumed he knew why. Moses had been in the news lately after the Pennsylvania Superior Court agreed to hear his argument regarding unconstitutional delay for his client, Keith Snyder, who had recently been accused of a murder more than eleven years earlier.

Moses picked up the phone. "I guess you're calling me about Snyder."

"No," Todd O'Malley responded. "I want to talk to you about Scher. I want you to talk to my brother. He's very ill and he's in need of some help trying this case."

John Moses had heard about the Scher case, and he was not interested in getting involved. He expected to be elected chairman of the board of Alsac/St. Jude Children's Hospital in Memphis in October, a position that required a good deal of time and travel. Besides, the fifty-one-year-old Moses was overloaded with work. In a redbrick turn-of-the-century building on a tree-lined street in downtown Wilkes-Barre, Moses's firm represented some four thousand clients including Blue Cross of Northeastern Pennsylvania, PG Energy, and the Pennsylvania state police.

Still, John Moses couldn't resist hearing more about the case. A meticulous student of law, the energetic Moses loved complicated legal issues. If he could help, with minimal inconvenience to his other commitments, he would.

"Have your brother come down," he told Todd O'Malley. "We'll talk about it."

The next day, Peter O'Malley drove to Wilkes-Barre and explained the situation, the twenty-year-old case, the arrest, the one million dollars bail. He told Moses that the doctor was struggling to raise bond, but the judge's stipulation that out-of-state property could not be used made it extremely difficult. O'Malley stressed that Scher was not in good health, that he needed to be released to support his family and be able to mount a proper defense.

John Moses listened intently but was still not swayed. "I'm not really interested, but I'm happy to help."

Peter O'Malley was persistent. "At least meet the guy." He handed Moses a thick file on the case.

Curiosity got the better of John Moses, and he agreed. The next day, he went to the Susquehanna County Jail and spoke to Stephen Scher. The doctor told him he couldn't understand why he was still in jail.

John Moses couldn't either. He'd read Judge Seamans's decision and was puzzled. Moses himself was on the Pennsylvania Supreme Court Criminal Rules Committee and knew firsthand that the edict had been changed—property out of the Commonwealth of Pennsylvania could indeed be posted as bond.

"Tell you what I'll do," he told Scher. "I'll make no commitment about getting involved in this case. I can never guarantee what will happen, but I *can* guarantee that the Supreme Court will make a decision about the bail hearing."

Driving back to Wilkes-Barre that day, Moses was determined to work out the bail issue. He decided he wasn't even going to charge Stephen Scher.

One thing I do know, he said to himself, are rules of criminal procedure and rules of evidence. This was an illegal order. No one knows how to bring it to the attention of the court.

Except John Moses. He immediately wrote a letter to the Superior Court explaining the situation and then began calling the court's prothonotary's office daily. Three days later, the attorney got a call from the clerk in the Superior Court: The Pennsylvania Superior Court in Philadelphia reduced Stephen Scher's bail to $750,000. More important, the court ruled that out-of-county property was permitted to be put up as bond.

The Schers and Peter O'Malley were astounded. But to those who knew John Moses, it didn't seem surprising.

Indeed, the Wilkes-Barre lawyer had an established reputation as someone who got things done by picking up the phone and calling the right people. In recent years, Moses had been instrumental in saving a historic theater in town by helping to raise more than three million dollars in a matter of days, and then he did all the legal work for free, overseeing the building's renovation into a performing arts center. Known for sending ties and scarves as Christmas gifts to a long list of friends and associates, his unpretentious style and knack for politicking earned him friends in high places, including judges in the state superior courts. Moses's supporters enjoyed his upbeat, fast-paced style—he loved a good joke, always grabbed the check at restaurants, and didn't like vacations because he preferred Wilkes-Barre to anyplace in the world.

He'd grown up in the town, behind his grandfather's dry goods store, the third of four boys. Moses worked after school throughout his youth and met his future wife, Joyce, when she and her mother were shopping at the supermarket where he was stocking shelves after school. He attended King's College, on the banks of the Susquehanna River in Wilkes-Barre, and left the area just once—to go to Villanova School of Law. Oddly, he was in the same graduating class as Marty Dillon but didn't remember ever meeting the young man.

He returned to Wilkes-Barre after graduation and built his practice, going into partnership with Charlie Gelso on a handshake agreement twenty-three years ago. The two owned the building together, divided the firm's work, and split the expenses. Gelso handled criminal cases filed in federal court; Moses took care of the state work.

Moses and his wife shunned a more affluent home in the mountains surrounding Wilkes-Barre in favor of a modest ranch-style house in the city, a mile east of his firm. The walls of the attorney's spacious office on the first floor of the brownstone were filled with framed photographs of him at black tie charity events and law conferences next to various politicians and celebrities including Hillary Clinton, Ted Kennedy, George Burns, and Bob Hope. Moses had some six hundred photos in his collection and had his secretary, Helen Barsh, rotate them every few months, leaving only family pictures and a portrait of his wife, Joyce, in place all the time. Laminated newspaper articles trumpeting his successful legal maneuvers over the years were displayed on the walls as well.

The latest triumph was especially pleasing to John Moses, certainly bound for a place on his wall. On July 29, 1996, Stephen Scher was released from jail. He'd posted $115,000 bail, Pat's cousin Joanne Kuehner posted her $450,000 house in the area, and Pat's relatives Joseph and Mary Castrogiovanni, their $105,000 home in Dunmore.

When John Moses met him at the jail, Stephen Scher hugged him and immediately asked the attorney to represent him. Moses was wary—he knew that Peter O'Malley was still involved in the case, and he did not want to sit as second chair.

"I'm fifty-one," Moses told Scher bluntly. "Been there, done that. I don't need the business. I've got a problem managing my practice as it is."

But Stephen Scher insisted that Moses could put together the defense team he wanted. The doctor was resolute—he wanted John Moses.

The attorney wavered. "Steve, I'll do anything I can to help you. Why do you want me? Why is it so important?"

Stephen Scher had a feeling about John Moses, and so did Pat. They were struck by the fact that Scher had spent forty days in prison and a man named Moses led him out. Even the attorney's commitment to St. Jude's Hospital seemed significant to the Schers; they told him they had purchased a stained-glass window of St. Jude for their church in Lincolnton.

It was a sign. Stephen and Pat Scher were sure of it.

Despite a healthy self-esteem, John Moses worried about the Schers' expectations. "I'm not in the insurance business," he often reminded his clients. Indeed, the attorney knew to be careful about what he said in the initial stages of a defense. He'd been practicing law long enough to know that if he ultimately lost a case, he'd be blamed. If he won, the defendants generally assumed they'd have won no matter who their lawyer was.

Besides, Moses wanted to be sure of what he was getting into. "I have enough money," he told Scher. "I only want to get involved if I know you're innocent."

Stephen Scher fervently insisted he was. The lawyer said he would think about it.

At home, Joyce Moses was less than enthusiastic. She reminded him of all he had going on. He was in the office by five most mornings, and at home he generally stayed up past midnight, working.

"You don't really want to do this, do you?" Joyce Moses asked.

Moses's twenty-one-year-old son, Peter, had the opposite reaction. The young man was a senior at King's College and applying to law school. "Dad, this is a great case. You have to take it."

John Moses was torn. Defending a murder suspect

meant practically living with the defendant. "There's nothing worse than spending time with someone you can't stand," he told his wife. "But I don't have that with Scher. I really believe he's innocent. And I like the guy."

He made up his mind. The case was too good to pass up—if the Schers were willing to meet his price: around $500,000. He discussed it with Joyce. "If they're prepared to pay this fee, I'm in," he said. "If they can't, I'll be able to tell my grandchildren, 'You know, I could have had this case.' "

Moses concluded that he'd be satisfied whichever way it turned out. He wasn't eager to do all the work; at the same time the case presented a fascinating challenge.

Everything you'd want in a case is here, he thought. Issue of delay, people have died, the doctor who did the original autopsy, the coroner, the detective. I have a client, a doctor, who has a great reputation in New Mexico, North Carolina. There's a hint of prejudice, that he's Jewish. The community's been worked on for twenty years; everything's been twisted.

On the Sunday after Stephen Scher was released from prison, Pat Scher came to Wilkes-Barre to meet with Moses. When she arrived, the attorney told her his fee to represent Stephen Scher. Pat Scher did not pause. "We'll find a way to do it," she said.

By this time, the Schers had already sold their home in Lincolnton, the brick split level Pat had liked so much, and were renting a house on the lake in a nearby town. Stephen Scher was forced to sell the Mercedes, too.

They would do whatever they had to. They believed John Moses was Stephen Scher's only hope.

Once he took on Scher's defense, John Moses filed a Petition for Delivery of Evidence, asking for the photographs of the scene of death, information regarding measurements taken at the scene of the tree stump allegedly stained with blood, studies of terrain at the scene of death, description of person, shotgun, clothing of Dillon, clothing of Scher, statement reports from the FBI, and forensic reports.

He began meeting with forensic and ballistic experts, put together a witness list, and retained a Harrisburg investigator, Skip Gochenaur, whom he'd worked with on several previous murder cases, to conduct interviews. In truth, Moses hoped to avoid a trial altogether. In the first few months, he focused on the issue of delay—that his client could not properly defend himself against twenty-year-old charges for myriad reasons.

At the same time, if his efforts to avoid a trial failed, he hoped to soften Stephen Scher's image in Susquehanna County. Before Moses had taken over, Peter O'Malley had arranged for Pat Scher to give an interview to a reporter, Kevin Ellis, from the *Binghamton Press & Sun Bulletin*. They met over the summer in the allergy office in Lincolnton days before Scher's release. Pat described her family's agony.

"I thought when Marty died there wasn't any greater pain but this is worse," she was quoted saying. "My children are grown and I see the pain in their adult eyes and I can't take it away. They see the same in mine, and we're all helpless. . . . To find every detail of your life speculated about, without any facts being put forth, and when you see events of your life put in a chronology so that there's only one conclusion, it probably hurts more than anyone could imagine. . . . Twenty years ago I had just lost my husband. He went to work one day and never came home. There were people in positions of authority. They made their decisions, and I had no reason to question it. I was much more concerned with my babies.''

Pat showed the reporter calla lilies in a plastic cup, a gift from a patient who knew they were her husband's favorite.

''The people of this community are so incredible I don't know what I and Stephen have ever done to deserve them,'' Pat said. ''I don't think I have enough days in my life to thank them. But I will thank them every day of my life.''

She told the reporter that she didn't understand Larry and Jo Dillon. ''I don't wish them any more pain,'' she said. ''We have all suffered enough. They lost a child and there couldn't be anything worse than that. But why would you let hate overtake all that is good? Why would you throw away your son's children, the only living part of your child? How could you do that? If someone could help me understand it would all be easier to take.''

Just after Labor Day 1996, a week-long preliminary hearing was held before New Milford District Justice Peter Janicelli. John Moses immediately raised the issue of unreasonable and unnecessary delay.

''We believe it is fundamentally unfair, when there is no reason for a delay, to cause a delay of 20 years in the interim where people die, where memories dim, where evidence is not properly preserved and then to require the defendant to defend himself,'' he charged. ''That is the sum and substance of the due process argument, Your Honor. My position is that the delay of that period of time was unreasonable and unneccesary, that the delay affected a set of circumstances which prevents this defendant from obtaining a fair proceeding. What are those circumstances? Witnesses die. The coroner in this case is dead. The original people that worked on the case are dead. Memories dim. We're talking about 20 years.''

Senior Deputy Attorney General Robert Campolongo pointed out that there is no statute of limitations on murder. ''It is not a violation of due process to take a murder charge, however later, because the law does not forget about murders. No matter how much time goes by, if a human life has been taken and evidence is developed, however late, that someone deliberately, maliciously took a human life, then that person is prosecuted under the law, regardless of the passage of time. Nothing can be clearer than that.''

He added that Pat Scher caused the more recent delays by contesting the exhumation of her first husband's body. ''We had to fight tooth and nail every inch of the way in order to get access to the body over her strenuous objection, and learned and numerous counsel that she had employed to take this matter all the way up to the Superior Court to impede the progress of our investigation,'' Campolongo told Janicelli.

The Commonwealth presented a series of witnesses. Dr. Isadore Mihalakis testified, and so did Frank Zanin. The former records and identification officer, now retired, talked about the battle to convince his superiors to look into Martin Dillon's death.

''For years every time we had a change of personnel, higher-up personnel at Dunmore, I would go to the incoming lieutenants in the crime division,'' he told the court. "It was always, 'Yeah. That needs to be worked on.' Period. And they just left it go. Left it go. Until finally in 1989 after it wasn't just me then, it was the Dillon family through attorney Loftus, also pushing on them that they finally started to take action and get work done."

On cross-examination, John Moses asked Zanin why he didn't protest in writing.

"You can lodge them written, you can lodge them verbal, you can speak until you're blue in the face sometimes," Zanin responded.

Former district attorney Ed Little also testified. He told the court that in 1976 coroner John Conarton was "hell bent accidental" and that he did not have sufficient evidence to prosecute. Larry Kelly, the DA from 1980 until 1988, testified briefly, saying that he never found a file on the Dillon case, nor did anyone ever ask him to investigate the death as a possible homicide.

In the end, the district judge was not swayed by Moses's arguments regarding the delay issue and ruled that there was sufficient evidence for trial. Over the next few months, John Moses attempted to halt a trial by filing various motions, all of which were denied. At pretrial hearings in May 1997, Judge Kenneth Seamans ruled against Moses's motion to suppress Scher's statement to Jock Collier and his requests for a change of venue and to dismiss all charges.

A trial date of June 9, 1997, was scheduled, but Moses requested a postponement and it was granted. The new trial date was firm: September 10, 1997, on the second-floor courtroom of the Susquehanna County Court of Common Pleas.

During the summer, Moses struggled to organize his defense strategy, but his client's version of the shooting did not jibe with the state forensic pathologists', who were not convinced that the hole in Dillon's chest had been the result of a close contact wound. Even worse, none of the ballistics experts hired by Scher would dispute the FBI report that the doctor's boots contained high-velocity blood spatter at trial. Given that Scher maintained he was more than 150 feet away at the time of the shotgun blast, it didn't look good.

The angle of the wound was another problem. If Martin Dillon didn't trip and fall on Scher's shotgun, there was only one other possibility that might save Stephen Scher: that the lawyer had committed suicide.

In May, Moses arranged for Scher to meet with Dr. Richard Fishbein, a psychiatrist, to discuss Marty Dillon's temperament and mood at the time of his death. In a two-hour interview, Scher related that Marty had been depressed for several years, and he even claimed that the lawyer had once confided in him that he'd thought of driving off a cliff. Scher also told Fishbein that Marty drank excessively and that he'd given the lawyer a prescription for antidepressants.

Dr. Fishbein then asked to speak to Pat, who concurred that her former husband had been unstable. She said that Marty took a lot of Tylenol for persistent head- and backaches and antacids for stomach pain. She added that he had a low tolerance for frustration and in the last few months of his life seemed tired and depressed, snapping at the children and at her. When the doctor asked what Marty's relationship with Stephen Scher had been, Pat said, "They enjoyed each other's company and they were close."

For Pat Scher it seemed like a lifetime ago, her marriage to Dillon. Now, there was only one goal—to save Stephen Scher from going to jail.

As the trial date neared, locals in Montrose prepared for a flood of media. The county arranged to have the courtroom painted. The Public Avenue Deli braced for a busy fall. And the main hotel in town, Montrose House, turned away dozens of requests for reservations—almost all twelve of its rooms had been booked months earlier by Robert Campolongo and his team of assistants and investigators. John Moses and his assistants, Kevin Beals and Tom Specht, rented a house across the street from the borough police station and set up an office with charts and computers in the living room.

The trial was expected to last from four to six weeks. Just days before jury selection, Stephen Scher and John Moses sat down to review what they had. A decision had already been made: The defense would concede that there had been a sexual relationship between Scher and Pat Dillon. The prosecution's army of witnesses who had lived on Kelly Street or worked in Montrose General Hospital would surely sway the jury anyway. It was better, Moses believed, to admit to the affair and possibly drain some momentum out of the prosecution's case.

There was another reason John Moses wanted to stress the defense's honesty with the jury. If he could convince the twelve men and women that what they would hear was the truth—even if it seemed detrimental to the case—he believed they had their best chance.

Stephen Scher must have realized that his account of what happened on June 2, 1976, would not suffice. In the days before the trial, undoubtedly under extreme pressure, he finally broke. For the first time in twenty-one years, he admitted that he'd lied about what happened at Gunsmoke.

The story was about to change. Again.

CHAPTER 20

On the morning of jury selection, Dr. Stephen Scher walked into the back entrance of the Susquehanna County Court of Common Pleas hand in hand with his stepdaughter, followed by his wife and Michael Dillon.

Suzanne had recently quit her job as a costume designer for Renaissance Festivals in Colorado Springs in order to be in Montrose, and Michael, who'd given up his motorcycle racing career a few years earlier, took the semester off from New Mexico State University, where he'd been studying business. The Schers' son Jonathan, now seventeen, remained in Lincolnton where he was a senior in high school, and friends of the couple assured them they would look after him. As for Pat's seventy-seven-year-old mother, she was too ill to come to Pennsylvania. Suffering from leukemia and diabetes, Laura Karveller remained in Las Cruces with her son, Robby, waiting for daily updates from Montrose.

Larry and Jo Dillon were in the courtroom, seated in the first row with Jo's cousins, Bill and Vonda Nash. Jo's former boss at Bendix, John Lynch, and his wife, Bernice, sat with the Dillons, as did Jo's niece, Shelly Wolfe, who had announced to her family that she planned to sit through the entire trial, leaving her husband in Delaware to care for their children. Joann Reimel did not attend the proceedings—she was on the witness list, and Robert Campolongo asked her to stay out of the courtroom.

On the first day, jurors were pared down to 168 from a list of 300 after mailed-in requests for excuses. Jurors filled the 180-seat courtroom so that the Schers were forced to sit behind Larry and Jo Dillon in the first row. As jurors were excused, the Schers quickly relocated to the opposite side of the courtroom.

Addressing the jurors, Senior Deputy Attorney General Robert Campolongo told them they had been chosen for high duty and it was their responsibility not to shirk it. His voice boomed in the high-ceilinged courtroom.

When it was his turn to speak, John Moses smiled engagingly. It was not his disposition to shout. He simply asked prospective jurors to be honest in the answers they gave.

The two lawyers asked questions about divorce, adultery, religion, hunting knowledge, experience with the criminal justice system, and if the jurors knew any people on the witness list. Two jurors were picked the first day; three the next. In a week's time

the twelve men and women who would determine
Stephen Scher's fate were ready.

Opening arguments in *The Commonwealth of Pennsylvania v. Stephen Barry Scher* began on the chilly
morning of September 22, 1997. The Schers passed
television cameras in the lobby of the 140-year-old
courthouse and proceeded to the stairs, Suzanne leading the way. Peter O'Malley, who would sit in the
front row as an observer throughout much of the trial,
greeted them on the landing. Pat Dillon, in a black
pants suit with a green shirt, wore a cross around her
neck. She clasped O'Malley's hands warmly.

In the courtroom, the Scher family sat in the back
row. Suzanne put her arm around her stepfather, and
he sat wordlessly, his hand cupped to his mouth. At
nine-fifty, the court was ready. Dr. Scher walked
down the short aisle and took his place at the defense
table, next to Moses and his assistants. Pat and her
children took their places in the second row, next to
The Reverend Fallwell, who'd driven up from Lincolnton a few days earlier.

Judge Kenneth Seamans issued a strict admonition
to the reporters gathered in seats across from the witness box not to talk to jurors or to conduct any interviews in the courtroom. He ordered a ten-minute
recess, and then, at ten-forty-five, opening arguments
began.

The Commonwealth went first. Robert Campolongo rose and walked a few feet to face the five men
and seven women in the jury box. Campolongo told
the 12 Susquehanna County residents that he would
present them with a kind of table of contents, an easy

reference guide to the witnesses they would soon hear.

"When you hear the evidence, it will ring the bell of recognition in your mind and you will say, 'Ahh, here is another piece of the puzzle,' " he explained.

He gestured to the defense table and told them about the silver-haired, bespectacled man who faced them: the defendant, Stephen Scher, charged with first- and third-degree murder. Campolongo wasted no time in reminding the jury that it was the first charge, the intentional murder charge, that he planned to prove. He outlined the case, the blood-spattered sunglasses and ear protectors, the angle of the wound, the doctor's gun.

Next he talked about the affair. "This defendant wanted to see Martin Dillon dead, and nothing but dead would do," he said in a menacing voice.

Then, in the quiet of the courtroom, Campolongo shouted: "The law never forgets. Never!"

His voice returned to normal. "There is nothing more precious than human life. There is no statute of limitations on murder. The law sooner or later has its say."

He recounted a bit about Martin Dillon, whose whole future lay ahead of him. A simple man, he called him, who loved his children and his wife, who always thought the best of people, a man who didn't want to believe there were people who had evil in their hearts even though on the outside they were full of smiles, with butter melting in their mouth.

His reference to Stephen Scher was clear. He told the jury that Stephen Scher and Patty Dillon "started having an affair, a sexual affair, but the sexual affair was not a particularly discreet one," he explained.

"I'm sorry to say neither of them cared a bit about Martin Dillon. This defendant just didn't care. This affair was in full force about a year before the death of Martin Dillon."

Campolongo gave them a sampling of what was to come: coworkers who saw them kissing; neighbors who watched the doctor's car come and go like clockwork, missing Marty Dillon by a few carefully calculated minutes; nurses who witnessed Scher's hands on Patty; their closed-door rendezvous in room 13.

"It's not just the affair, it's that it was conducted in this open, blatant manner," Campolongo said. "They had no regard.

" 'He was my best friend,' " he said, mimicking Scher. "You have to ask yourself whether your best friend has sex with your wife. . . . He thinks he can do whatever he pleases and it doesn't matter who knows it. He's above it all. It also shows you when he says 'Martin Dillon is my best friend.' This is evidence to show that's a lie. If that's a best friend, what is an enemy?"

In the quiet of the courtroom, Robert Campolongo thundered on. "This defendant wanted to marry Patty Dillon. He wanted to take her away, to go to another state. He believes in the religion of Stephen Scher. 'Whatever I want I get in one way or another.' He himself admitted he was an amoral person and he would do whatever he had to to get what he wanted. That was his religion. The religion of me, the hell with you."

Campolongo's vitriolic opening arguments did not spare Patricia Dillon. As she sat motionless, her children flanking her, her minister at the end of the row, she listened to the prosecuting attorney outline her flaws. Yet clearly he was less critical of her, of the weakness of a woman who had been raised to believe that she deserved the best and that marrying a physician was her right.

"She said to one person, 'I love them both and I don't know what to do,' " Campolongo said. "She was up there in la la land. In a way she had been manipulated by this defendant. She forgot about her husband, about her loyalty, how bad her husband was looking in the town. She forgot, in her weakness. She didn't know what to do. She couldn't go against her religion. She couldn't face up to her family."

He told the jury that Pat Dillon had told Stephen Scher just weeks before her husband's death that she could not leave town with him, that she must stay with Marty. And at some point, she conveyed this message to Marty as well.

Campolongo seemed to wonder aloud how this announcement was taken by the young Montrose attorney. "What was going through Martin Dillon's mind this whole period? He was a man who just couldn't believe something like this could happen. 'My wife, two little kids, how could this be?' He engaged in denial. He couldn't believe that anyone would do this. Finally the evidence became so overwhelming people were talking, 'Look, you've got to do something,' and he went into the second phase. 'Maybe it will disappear.' He wasn't a violent man. He wasn't a confrontational man. He was a gentle man."

Marty Dillon, he told the jurors, had issued an ultimatum to his wife, and she had said that she would choose him.

"Stephen Scher could not accept this," Campolongo told the jury. "This is someone telling him that

he could not have what he wanted. This was a violation of the first tenet of his religion of self—that he
could not have what he wanted.''

Campolongo walked the jury through the events of
June 2, 1976. He talked about how Marty Dillon was
uncomfortable about going trap shooting alone with
Stephen Scher, how he invited numerous friends,
practically pleading for them to join him. But when
they did not, Marty went anyway, not believing that
any harm could come to him at the hands of Stephen
Scher.

Campolongo told the jury that Marty Dillon, his ear
protectors and sunglasses on, was preparing to operate
the skeet machine. The prosecutor raised an imagi-
nary gun.

''The defendant—'I will get what I want' . . . and
Boom!'' Campolongo's voice exploded through the
courtroom. ''He's down. The blood impact spatters
out of his chest onto the log he was near, he falls on
top of the clay pigeon he had in his hand. High-speed
spatter. The defendant, only a few feet away, pointed
it right at his heart. Rolled him over. 'Let me untie
his shoe.' Took his gun, threw it up ahead of the
body. . . . Then he went into his Hollywood act.''

As jurors listened intently, Campolongo continued.
''We will prove this man turns on and off like a
switch. The pinpoints of blood put him right there.
Make him a liar, make him the murderer that he is.
. . . This was no accident, no suicide. It was murder.
Somebody else shot him. The only somebody else
that was there was this defendant. He was the one
with the motive, with the number 4 shot. An 8 shot
probably isn't good enough. For an accident, you only
have one shot. If you've got only one shot, you've

got to make it count. It's got to be 100 percent. You've got to make sure this person doesn't live to tell the tale.''

It was a compelling start. The court recessed for lunch, and then it was John Moses's turn.

He quickly attempted to defuse the emotion stirred by Robert Campolongo. In a quiet voice, Moses greeted the jurors and stood at the lectern, explaining that what they'd just heard was a statement, not evidence. He challenged remarks Campolongo had made, pointing out that the deputy attorney general had never spoken to Stephen and Pat Scher or to Michael and Suzanne Dillon.

"This courtroom is a temple of justice," he told them. "... We can't take liberties with the truth and expect the justice system to work. ... The defense is clear. It is direct and it is honest. We believe the evidence in this case clearly demonstrates that the defendant is innocent. Stephen Scher did not murder Martin Dillon. ... The defense in this case is three pronged: honesty, the evidence and the presumption of innocence. Sometimes it's not easy to be honest. Sometimes it's pretty hard. But we have promised you that we will be honest. Let's start now."

To the surprise of many in the courtroom, John Moses told the jury that Stephen Scher and Pat Dillon were having an affair during the last year of her marriage. He told them they would hear that for themselves, from Stephen Scher.

"He will admit to you that he had sexual relations with Pat Dillon while she was married to Martin Dillon," he said. "Despite the fact that there is no direct evidence of that activity in this case, we'll tell you now. We'll also tell you that Dr. Scher had sexual relations with other women at the same time. You will get the truth from us, warts and all. . . . Let me make it perfectly clear, we will not pin a star or a medal on Stephen Scher for his sexual activity.''

Moses went on to discuss the experts the defense would present, Dr. Cyril Wecht, Dr. Michael Baden, and Dr. John Shane. He told them they would learn that the Winchester is dangerously designed; their expert examined the very gun that caused Martin Dillon's death and found it was filled with dirt and grime, increasing the possibility of an accident.

He poked at Campolongo's style. ''I'm not going to holler at you,'' he told the jury. ''I'm not going to scold you. I'm going to ask you to look at the evidence.''

Moses recounted what went on after Dillon's death, how Dr. Grace performed an autopsy, and coroner Conarton ruled it an accident. He pointed out that the amended death certificate in 1995 was made by someone who wasn't there in 1976. ''That person was not at the scene, did not talk to Stephen Scher, was not at the autopsy. The people who were at the scene and at the autopsy are now dead, except for Mr. Little. . . . Twenty years ago when the evidence was fresh, people were alive, people remembered things.''

He told them not only to look at the evidence but also to consider the lack of evidence. ''Yes, that was Stephen Scher's gun, but the evidence in this case will show that the guys who went to Gunsmoke always exchanged guns. On the day of this incident Martin Dillon didn't take any of his guns—he took Kendall Strawn's gun. This gun was full of muck and junk. . . . Bring your common sense to the courtroom.''

He told them that Scher had desperately tried to

help his friend. "Dr. Scher is dedicated to saving lives," Moses said earnestly. "The evidence will show that Stephen Scher attempted to save the life of Martin Dillon. Mr. Russin will tell you that when he saw Dr. Scher there was blood all over his hands and mouth and the ambulance attendant will say she saw him over the body of Martin Dillon and there was blood all over."

The attorney then related details of Stephen Scher's life, of his early years in Canada, the family's move to Florida, his father's tragic death, his mother's remarriage. He told the jury of the defendant's lifelong desire to be a physician, to save lives, and how he pursued that dream even after his mother's death, when he and his sister were left alone in the world. Moses described how Stephen Scher had worked his way through school, how he'd married Ann Elias and moved to an Indian reservation in New Mexico. The marriage, he told the jury, deteriorated, and the couple separated. Then, on June 2, Martin Dillon died.

"Ladies and gentlemen, shortly after June 2, Pat Scher moved to Philadelphia and Steve moved back to New Mexico," he said firmly. "Different parts of the country."

He said that it was two years later that the couple got together. "They moved to New Mexico," he explained. "The household was Steve Scher, Pat, Michael and Suzanne. They will take the witness stand and they will tell you about the home life and how Stephen Scher raised them."

He told the jury to look carefully at the facts. "I can ask you not to be distracted. I can ask you to concentrate on the crimes charged. It's Stephen Scher's right and it's my obligation. . . . I promise you honesty. There's only one person who can tell you what happened on June 2, 1976, only one . . .''

He pointed to his client, who sat expressionless, his gaze on the jury box. ''And he sits here.''

''Stephen Scher,'' Moses said softly. ''And he sits there cloaked with the presumption of innocence and does not have to take the stand, but this is the search for the truth and he will waive that right and he will take the witness stand and he will tell you exactly what happened on June 2, 1976.''

CHAPTER 21

In the days that followed, one by one, nurses, former neighbors, and friends stepped up to the witness box and shared their knowledge of the love affair between Dr. Stephen Scher and the young Patty Dillon.

Elaine Henninger talked about seeing Scher's car pass her house every morning, en route to 7 Kelly Street, and spoke of the evenings Pat and Steve locked themselves into room 13. In a moving videotape, Sandra Jean Price, now suffering from advanced breast cancer, testified from her hospital room in soft, measured words about the breast-grabbing incident.

Jo Ann Warner Leonard, who'd been the receptionist at the hospital, testified about the many times Scher gave Pat's number when he was on call. At one point, Campolongo asked her about the day Scher abruptly left the hospital. Jo Ann started to explain that it had been after he'd learned of Suzanne Dillon's

birth, but John Moses loudly objected, and the judge
sustained the motion.

Jo Ann looked at Pat, shifting in her seat, and
thought she appeared uncomfortable. Jo Ann then
looked at Dr. Scher, and their eyes met. She felt a
chill from his glare. They remember, Jo Ann thought.
And so do I.

For the most part, John Moses did not try to refute
the testimony of the women from Montrose General;
after all, the defense had conceded the affair. But he
did attempt to undo the damage done by Jocelyn
Richards, the nurse's aide who told jurors about the
conversation she'd had with Dr. Stephen Scher, when
he disclosed he was an atheist and said his philosophy
of life was that he got what he wanted.

Moses repeatedly pressed Richards whether they
often joked at the hospital, and perhaps those remarks
were made in a lighthearted manner. But Jocelyn
Richards couldn't be swayed. She remembered the
steel gray eyes of Dr. Stephen Scher when he spoke,
how his words had surprised her, staying vivid in her
mind for more than two decades.

"It was a serious conversation," she told Moses
unequivocally.

Under direct examination by Robert Campolongo,
Richards testified about walking in on Pat and Scher
kissing in the drug room. She told the court what she
remembered and why she would never forget. "It was
very improper," she said firmly. "I was stunned. Of
course it stayed in my mind. It was not something
you'd see in a work place."

Betty Williams also testified about seeing Scher
with his hands up Pat Dillon's skirt in the drug room.
During his cross-examination Moses asked her why

she did not confront the doctor and nurse.

"I was shocked by what I had seen," Williams said. "I thought it was inappropriate activity in a professional institution."

"Did you ever file a formal complaint?" Moses challenged.

"No," Williams admitted. There was a pause. "Except," she said finally, "in my own mind."

Justine Jenner testified about the day Scher came to her home asking about Catholicism, wanting to know why Patty couldn't practice her religion if she went away with him. She told the court how much she'd admired Dr. Scher, that she didn't tell anyone for many years because she didn't want to get him in trouble. She confessed that her husband was not happy about her involvement in the trial but that she felt it was something she had to do.

When it was Carol Gazda's turn, the former Silver Lake Ambulance Squad volunteer took the stand, a bit nervous. For days before the trial began she'd repeatedly asked Lieutenant Hacken if she really was necessary for the prosecution's case. She told him that she worried that she might look silly on the stand.

Hacken tried to reassure her. "It's a very important piece of evidence," he explained. "You just don't realize it."

Gazda's testimony took just a few minutes. On cross-examination, Moses tried to defuse her story, implying that it was surely possible for someone to become more emotional when other people were around.

On the fourth day of testimony, Kerry Graham told jurors that Marty had been his best friend, and he recounted the day they went skeet shooting at Gunsmoke, when Marty had cried and confessed that his marriage was in trouble. The next witness was Kendall Strawn, who told jurors that Marty Dillon had been like a brother to him. He revealed Marty's plan to give Pat an ultimatum, and later Scher's reaction at the surprise party, the look Strawn could never forget.

The next day, at the end of week two of the trial, Ann Vitale and Andrew Russin testified. Ann spent almost two hours on the stand, relaying details of her marriage, of the trip to Wyoming where she'd seen her husband massaging Pat's legs, of the time she says Scher admitted to her he was in love with Pat. Over repeated objections by John Moses, Ann brought up the pills left in the bathroom on the day Scher went on an out-of-town trip with Patty Dillon.

When Ann Vitale was excused, there was a long pause as the court waited for the next witness: Andrew Russin.

Now eighty-six years old and a widower, Russin had gotten up early that day and driven his 1996 Geo Tracker to the courthouse in Montrose. As he pulled out of his driveway, he'd passed the white Jeep he'd driven up to Gunsmoke that day twenty-one years before. It was all rusted now and covered with weeds.

When Russin arrived at the courthouse he wasn't sure where he was supposed to wait. Heck, I'm here, he thought. I might as well listen to the case. He looked around, wondering if he would get into trouble. If I don't belong, he decided, they'll tell me.

From the balcony, he listened to the testimony of Ann Scher and leaned over to watch a court sketch-artist drawing. During a short recess, Robert Campolongo came up to the balcony. "You're up next," he said.

Andrew Russin nodded. He didn't know whether that meant he should go downstairs or wait. So he waited.

When it was time, Judge Kenneth Seamans caught sight of him in the balcony and waved to him.

The court waited as the elderly man approached the witness box. When asked by Campolongo for his age, Andrew Russin said, "If I live till December, I'll be 87."

For the first time in the two-week proceeding, Pat Scher smiled.

Russin told of the evening of June 2, how Scher had come to his home to tell of a shooting accident. He said Scher had been unemotional until he swung the gun at the tree.

On cross-examination, John Moses suggested that Russin had spoken to an investigator hired by Peter O'Malley two years earlier and had told him that Scher had been distraught and emotional at the scene. Andrew Russin shook his head. He didn't remember saying that, he told Moses. He didn't remember that at all.

When he was finished testifying, Andrew Russin drove home. He'd been confused by some of the questions he was asked. It had happened so very long ago.

But there are some things, the elderly man thought, you don't forget.

For the next week, a series of expert witnesses took the stand. Trooper Hairston testified, as did Frank Zanin. The statement Scher gave to the state police and to Jock Collier was read into evidence. The clothing, the Winchester, and the spent magnum load were shown to the jury. When large photographs of the body of Martin Dillon were displayed, Suzanne Dillon bowed her head.

Dr. Isadore Mihalakis spent more than a day on the witness stand and endured intense cross-examination by John Moses. The attorney struggled to cast doubt on the doctor's contention that the gunshot had been from at least three feet away and that there were no powder burns to suggest a contact wound.

But Mihalakis was resolute. "The wound cannot possibly under any stretch of the imagination be a contact wound, period," he announced.

Throughout the trial, Larry and Jo Dillon kept to a routine. Every morning, Bill and Vonda Nash picked them up at Gunsmoke for the drive to Montrose, and twice a week Jo first attended seven o'clock service at St. Josephine Catholic Church. The foursome arrived at the courthouse by eight-thirty and then met John Lynch, Jo's former boss at Bendix, and his wife who drove almost an hour every day from Nichols. While the couples waited in Sheriff Dick Pelicci's office until it was time to go upstairs, Bill Nash walked over to the Public Avenue Deli and gave owner Beverly Kinsey their lunch order.

The Dillons tried not to bump into the Schers coming into the courthouse. Their grandchildren did not speak to them, and it was painful to pass them in the halls. Once, early in the trial, Bill Nash approached Michael Dillon. "I'm glad to see you, Mike," he said earnestly. "I wish it was under better circumstances."

But the young man quickly turned away. "I don't think you and I should talk anymore," he said quietly.

During the lunch breaks, the Dillons, Nashes, and Lynches went to the Dillons' home at 27 Lincoln Avenue, and after court ended for the day they returned there again for coffee and to discuss the day. Then the Nashes drove Larry and Jo back to Gunsmoke, where they generally lived until winter set in.

The Schers and the Dillon children stayed with Pat's relatives in the area. They, too, had their supporters. The Reverend Farwell was on hand for the first week, and different friends and relatives stopped by throughout the proceedings. Pat's aunt Cecilia Dilello attended every day. Scher's cousin from New Jersey spent more than a week at the trial, and his sister, Susan, attended as well. Stephen Scher's cousin Dorothy Isan and her husband, Frank, spent several weeks in court.

In early October, the prosecution rested, and it was John Moses's turn. He called his first witness: Dr. Stephen Scher.

CHAPTER 22

Every seat in the courtroom was filled when Stephen Scher rose from the long oak defense table, walked to the witness box, and was sworn in. For the first time since the trial began, his wife and stepchildren were not in their usual seats in the second row. John Moses had asked them to wait outside; all three might be called later to testify.

Under direct examination, Stephen Scher, his voice measured and calm, began by carefully recounting his early years growing up in Toronto and Florida, the death of his parents, his medical training, and his marriage.

He told the jury that his relationship with Ann ultimately dissolved; he was working too much, and he and his wife drifted apart. He admitted having an affair with Pat but insisted they weren't in love at the time; it was only a sexual relationship. He told the jury he wasn't interested in getting involved with anyone—he was just emerging from a bad marriage.

Then Scher began to talk about June 2, 1976. He said it had been Marty who'd arranged the skeet shooting outing and that after the various friends dropped out, Scher said he hadn't even wanted to go at all—it was cold and overcast that day. But he explained that Marty had shown up at his house in the BMW and had already bought hamburger meat for a barbecue and didn't want to waste it. And so, Scher told the jury, they went.

Stephen Scher described the drive to Gunsmoke and how they shot the clay pigeons for a while. He said they discussed Marty's upcoming trial and Scher's plan to visit a friend in Knoxville.

Then Stephen Scher told the jury a story that no one had heard before. He claimed that Marty Dillon's mood changed abruptly. Without warning, Dillon confronted him about the affair.

"He said, 'Ann came to me and told me that you told her you loved Pat. When did that happen?'" Scher explained, "I walked over to him. I said, 'It doesn't matter when it happened. Do you believe her?' He said, 'I don't know, she's crazy. I don't know. All the rumor and gossip in town. My father's breathing down my neck about the gossip. I need to know.' He looked at the ground, like he didn't want to know. He looked up at me and said, 'I have to know. Are you and Pat having an affair?' I had to tell him the truth. He was looking me in the eye. I said, 'Yes. We're having not a love affair, a physical affair.' He was very anxious, very upset. I don't remember his exact words, how he phrased questions. I don't remember the order. He wanted to know how did this start. I told him, it just happened. Pat and I

worked close together. It just happened. He put his
hands over his ears. He rocked. He asked how long
had it been going on. I said, about a year. 'How often
were you screwing my wife?' Five or six times, the
last time in April. He wanted to know where. 'Are
you doing this in my house, in one of my cars, in the
hospital?' he wanted to know. I said, 'No. We would
go to a hotel.' He said, 'How could this have happened to me?' I said, 'Marty, I've seen you and your
family. I've watched your reaction to your wife and
kids. You show more reactiveness, more responsive-
ness to your father, to your practice, show more re-
sponsiveness to your damn BMW than you do to your
family. Maybe Pat was just lonely.' He said, 'Why
doesn't she tell me?' I said, 'She probably does, she
probably has. You just don't care.' I wasn't looking
at him. I said, 'You know, this is as much your fault
as it is anybody's.' ''

There wasn't a sound in the courtroom.

Scher continued. ''I heard a yell. He had the gun,
I knew I had to get that gun away. I didn't know what
he was going to do with it. I grabbed the gun, we
struggled, the gun went off and he turned white. . . .
I turned him over, punched his chest . . . I took off his
glasses and earmuffs. I pinched his nose. I started
screaming, 'Marty, don't die. Stop. Marty, don't.' He
was dead. I panicked. All of a sudden I got this feeling of panic, of aloneness. I was all alone. I was
afraid. I didn't know what to do. I was pacing around,
moaning. 'Marty, why did you have to do this?' . . .
I was a mess. My whole insides were in turmoil. . . .
I felt afraid. I was horrified. I was thinking, 'How can
I tell anybody this accident happened like this and
have anybody believe me?' With all the rumors that

were going on, me, being a relative newcomer to the area and Marty's father is the mayor. I was the only Jew in town. I felt I couldn't tell anybody. . . . I was messed up emotionally. I walked around some more. I had to sort things out. How can I tell people what happened? I decided since it was an accident, I was going to make it into another accident. I couldn't face the public, telling them the truth. I had to make something up, another accident. I made up a story about him running with the gun and tripping and falling. I was afraid I would be convicted and I'd never be able to practice medicine again so I made up that story and took the gun, wiped off the barrel with a handkerchief, put it back in my pocket. I put the gun with the muzzle facing his head. I untied his shoelace.''

Stephen Scher told of driving to Andrew Russin's place, sobbing, begging Russin to return with him to Gunsmoke. He explained how when he saw the gun he went ballistic, smashing it against the tree. When Trooper Hairston and John Conarton arrived, Scher said he told them the story about Marty running after a porcupine and tripping and falling. Later that night, he told jurors, he described going to Pat's house and telling her, too, the story he'd concocted.

When he was finished testifying, Stephen Scher looked relieved. So did his attorney. Scher had done better than John Moses expected. The doctor had been earnest and calm throughout his testimony, looking directly at the jurors, making eye contact.

Still, Stephen Scher wasn't off the hook. Senior Deputy Attorney General Robert Campolongo had questions. Lots of them.

For several hours, Campolongo hammered away at all the lies Scher had told for the past twenty-one years—about the affair and all his versions of what happened at Gunsmoke.

But Stephen Scher was well-prepared. He told Campolongo that he lied for a reason—he didn't want to hurt Pat and the children.

"I couldn't tell the truth about what happened," he said. "How can you tell someone that you just had a discussion with her husband about their infidelities and there was a struggle with the gun, and the gun went off? That person would feel guilty. I couldn't allow that to happen. For 21 years I couldn't tell what happened. I kept it down inside. The lie became me, me became the lie."

When Campolongo grilled him about why he changed his story, Scher was ready for that, too.

"I was on trial for my life," he said. "I had to let it out. I couldn't keep it in anymore."

Campolongo scoffed at the doctor's testimony. He asked him about the discovery handed over to the defense team, all the interviews, all the information from experts showing that Scher was within a few feet of Martin Dillon when he died.

"At the time you made this decision to tell this latest story, you had already seen what we had that put you right there, blood on your boot, the hem of your pants," Campolongo charged. "Did you know we could prove that with scientific certainty?"

Stephen Scher looked confused. "I'm sorry," he told Campolongo politely. "Please repeat the question."

Robert Campolongo's anger showed. "Did you know we had you right next to Marty Dillon?" he thundered.

But Stephen Scher maintained his composure. "I

knew what the scientific evidence was but I did not come forward because of that,'' he said simply.

Campolongo continued to pound away at how Scher's story kept changing—on June 2 the doctor claimed Marty had been running toward the trailer, and two days later he said they were inside the trailer. The prosecutor sarcastically asked him if he had changed his story about not being able to see Marty only after he realized there was nothing to obstruct his view. ''When you were made aware there was a clear view, didn't you change your story?'' Campolongo demanded.

''Whether the story changed or not, it continued to be the same lie,'' Stephen Scher responded. ''I didn't know what I was saying.''

Under cross-examination, Scher denied telling Ann that he loved Patty Dillon, and he also refuted her claim that she'd seen him rubbing Pat's legs on the Wyoming trip the two couples took in the summer of 1975.

''Patricia Dillon had severe phlebitis,'' Scher explained. ''There was no reason for anybody to rub her legs.''

He also disputed Justine Jenner's testimony, saying he never asked his former patient about the rules of Catholicism, nor did he discuss taking Patty out of town.

Campolongo repeatedly referred to Scher's statements from the press conference at Peter O'Malley's, ticking off all the lies the doctor had told reporters. The prosecutor brought up the bitter words Scher had used to describe Larry Dillon, when he called Marty's father a liar and a vicious man.

Campolongo pointed to the seventy-seven-year-old

Larry Dillon, holding a cane, sitting in the front row. "You were impugning this man who lost his son, weren't you?" the prosecutor barked.

"I don't believe so," Scher said calmly.

When court finally recessed at four o'clock, the prosecution team met for several hours in their office on the third floor and later over dinner at Montrose House to discuss the next day's strategy. By morning, a decision was reached: Campolongo would end his cross-examination of Scher. As for the doctor's account of the shooting, the prosecutor would not even address it.

Stephen Scher, Campolongo grudgingly had to admit, was masterful at control. He was unshaken by the prosecutor's questions, unruffled by the intense pressure. Indeed, it was Robert Campolongo who was beginning to lose his composure. The deputy attorney general's fear was real: The longer Scher stayed on the witness stand, the more chance the doctor just might be believed.

When court opened the next morning, Campolongo announced that he had no further questions for the defendant.

Over the next week, John Moses's defense of Stephen Scher continued. The attorney called a reluctant Susan Strope to the stand. The former emergency medical technician was horrified when she learned that John Moses intended to call her as a defense witness. Strope believed that Dr. Scher was guilty of murder—the last thing she wanted to do was to help him.

But she'd been subpoenaed and had no choice. On the stand, Strope testified that she'd received the call about a shooting accident and she and her husband had rushed to the scene. She described how Stephen Scher had hugged a tree, crying, and that she'd given him a moist towelette to wipe the blood off his face and hands. Then she was asked about the twenty-minute drive to the hospital.

"I asked how he was," she said in a flat tone. "He said, 'I'm OK. I'm thinking about those little kids. I'm going to have to look after those little kids.'"

When Susan Strope finished, the trial recessed for lunch. She walked over to Larry and Jo Dillon, sheepishly shaking her head. Jo Dillon reached for her hand. "You did fine," she said warmly. "That was just fine."

The defense then called Norman Fiske, a sixty-eight-year-old friend of Scher's from New Milford.

"You know the kind of reputation Stephen Scher had for being peaceful and law-abiding?" Moses asked.

"He was peaceful, law-abiding," Fiske responded. "He had compassion with his patients."

Marie Hoffman testified that she had worked for five years for Stephen Scher at his New Milford office. The patients, she testified, all liked Dr. Scher. When she was excused from the witness stand, Hoffman walked over to the defense table, and she and Scher embraced.

Gary Passmore testified that he had been supposed to go to Gunsmoke on June 2 but canceled to have dinner with his wife for her birthday. Under questioning by John Moses, Passmore told the court that the men at Gunsmoke often borrowed each other's guns. It would not be unusual, he said, for Marty to have been using Scher's shotgun.

The defense called a battery of expert witnesses—

Dr. John Shane, Dr. Michael Baden, and Dr. Cyril Wecht. All three testified that the accident could have occurred as Scher now described it and refuted the prosecution's contention that the shot had been from several feet away. The defense also called George Fassnacht, a ballistics expert, who testified that the Winchester used in the shooting was a dangerous model and could have misfired. Under cross-examination by Campolongo, however, Fassnacht admitted that after repeated tests, the Winchester failed to discharge accidentally.

At one point during the medical testimony, however, Judge Seamans surprised the courtroom by recessing for the day before the lunch break. Curious reporters noticed that Larry and Jo Dillon remained in the courthouse, meeting with the prosecution team for most of the afternoon.

Rumors swirled that a plea bargain was in the works. Indeed, it was later confirmed that the prosecution offered Dr. Stephen Scher an opportunity to plead guilty to third-degree murder instead of risking a conviction on the highest count, intentional murder. Campolongo discussed it with Larry and Jo Dillon, and they had no objection. Judge Seamans made it clear that although he couldn't make any promises, he would consider leniency for the defendant, based on the doctor's years of service and his close ties to his family. The judge put the number of years Scher could expect to serve at around seven.

But Stephen Scher, with his wife and stepchildren's support, rejected the offer. All believed the jury would acquit him.

In the days following the plea offer, however, court watchers noticed a shift in John Moses's strategy. After a measured and carefully presented defense, the attorney called a woman who stunned the courtroom with her testimony.

Cindy Klein, who had been the Dillons' fifteen-year-old baby-sitter at the time of Marty's death, testified that a week before Marty's death, the young lawyer drove her home after she'd taken care of Michael and Suzanne for the evening. He was drunk, she claimed, and talkative. Klein told the jury that Marty Dillon confessed to her that Stephen Scher had been having an affair with his wife, and that Dillon planned to kill him. She said that Dillon told her he would take Scher to Gunsmoke, shoot him, and make it look like an accident. She alleged that Dillon told her he would be believed because his father was the mayor of Montrose, and Scher was the only Jew in town.

When Cindy Klein finished testifying, titters echoed through the courtroom, and Robert Campolongo barely bothered to cross-examine the young woman. In the second row, for the first time during the trial, Pat Scher began crying. If the courtroom spectators' response was an indication of what jurors were thinking, things did not look good for her husband.

Just before the defense rested, John Moses called Michael and Suzanne Dillon to the stand. On both occasions, after a sidebar conference with the attorneys, Judge Seamans ruled that neither would be permitted to testify. Their opinions on the kind of father Stephen Scher had been to them were not relevant to the case, he said.

But Moses wanted to be sure the jurors knew that Michael and Suzanne had been willing to speak on

behalf of Stephen Scher, and so both took the stand
for a few minutes before they were excused by the
judge. As Michael returned to his seat, he stopped by
his stepfather and handed him a medal of St. Jude
he'd been clutching. Scher smiled at his stepson and
placed the medal in his jacket pocket. Then Michael
passed his grandparents as he returned to his seat.

Jo Dillon called out softly to him. "Hello, Michael," she said.

He did not respond.

At one point, Lieutenant Frank Hacken also attempted to reach out to Michael. He'd spoken to him
on the phone once, early on in the investigation, and
Michael had expressed complete support for his stepfather. Hacken felt sorry for the young man. The children, he believed, were victims.

One afternoon, during a break, the lieutenant
walked over to Michael and held out his business
card. Hacken explained that he'd learned a lot about
Marty Dillon in the last year and if Michael ever
wanted to hear about it, he'd be happy to talk. "I
wouldn't say anything about your mother or your
stepfather," Hacken reassured him. "But if you want
to talk about your father, call."

But Michael Dillon shook his head, and refused the
card.

"No," he said and walked away.

CHAPTER 23

After the defense rested, the prosecution called several rebuttal witnesses, including Julie Ann Poff, Cindy Klein's sister. Poff had phoned Larry and Jo Dillon at home the day after she learned her sister had claimed Marty Dillon told her he'd planned to kill Stephen Scher. The young woman was crying.

"I can't understand her," Poff told Jo Dillon. "I don't know why she did that."

The Dillons asked her to get in touch with Robert Campolongo, and Poff agreed. When she spoke to the prosecutor, Poff said she would be willing to travel from her home in North Carolina to refute her sister's testimony in court.

On the stand, Poff said Cindy Klein shouldn't be believed. "She is not telling the truth. My sister has a hard time telling reality from the truth," she announced.

"How would you describe your sister's reputation for truthfulness?" Campolongo asked.

"Bad."

"Would you believe your sister Cindy Klein's testimony under oath?" the prosecutor continued.

Poff didn't hesitate. "No."

On cross-examination, John Moses suggested that Poff's testimony was the result of a falling-out with her sister. Poff denied it.

The next day, the prosecution rested.

On October 21, 1997, the trees throughout town in brilliant color, John Moses and Robert Campolongo each gave two-hour closing arguments. By now, the trial had been underway for six weeks.

John Moses spoke first. He told the seven women and five men on the jury that Stephen Scher was clearly not guilty of murder unless the prosecution had proved every element of the crime. He reminded them that he had promised them an honest defense.

"I told you this was a temple of justice and your job was the pursuit of justice," he said. "Put my feet to the fire. I told you that 20 years ago, this incident was an accident. . . . kept my word. The system's got to work. I can't make it work. Dr. Scher can't make it work. You can make it work."

He urged them to look at the evidence and to remember that the defendant had the presumption of innocence. "It's the right we hold sacred, that every man is innocent. Not that you think he did it, that he probably did it, that he did it beyond a reasonable doubt."

Moses attacked the prosecution's portrayal of his

client. "Who's on trial here, some demonic figure?" he asked.

He reminded the jury that Scher had been honest with them about the affair, but that they shouldn't forget that it had been just a physical relationship. After June 2, 1976, he pointed out, Scher and Pat Dillon went in different directions. "One went to New Mexico, one went to Philadelphia, undisputed." It was only later, he explained, that the couple fell in love. Consequently, Moses announced, there was no motive for murder.

The attorney reminded the jury of Scher's life— that he'd lovingly raised Michael and Suzanne and had adopted Jonathan.

He went on to attack Campolongo for not asking Scher about the shooting during the prosecutor's cross-examination. He suggested from that, the jury should draw its own conclusion.

"You had him right here," Moses said, glancing at the prosecutor. "It was the quietest moment of the trial. . . . Stephen Scher told one lie. He knew that his sexual relationship was what caused this altercation. He thought, 'I've got to make this look like an accident. They won't believe the way it happened because of the rumors.' . . . He lived with a lie for 21 years because of an extra-marital relationship. He felt the blame and shame for the affair . . . I am going to beg you to discuss the questions, to analyze, to challenge. . . . I ask you to stay on the track that will take you to justice. I ask you to keep the promise that you made . . . to acquit him unless the Commonwealth proves intentional, willful, beyond a reasonable doubt. . . . I pray you will keep your word."

During the lunch break, Robert Campolongo went

over his notes with Bob O'Hara, the thirty-five-year-old deputy attorney general assigned to help him with the case. O'Hara, a former assistant district attorney in Scranton for nine years, had kept a low profile throughout the proceedings, but had been extremely helpful to Campolongo, quietly pointing out discrepancies in Moses's witnesses, suggesting effective arguments to the jury, and helping to calm his temperamental boss. Campolongo knew he wouldn't have had nearly as strong a presentation without the young lawyer.

When court resumed, Campolongo faced the jury. He told them that after hearing John Moses's closing arguments he thought he'd been listening to a different case. He asked jurors to examine the mind of the defendant.

"Go through the facts, particularly as they apply to the expert witnesses," he urged the jurors. "In this case we have the testimony of common sense. Why does he do the kinds of things he does? Watch how the story changes to fit the evidence. It paints this defendant into a corner. . . . We had him six ways from Sunday and he knew it. That's when the story changed. Irrefutable evidence of blood spatter that was turned over to them. It made it scientifically impossible to dispute . . . He was there. He had to be there."

The prosecutor scoffed at Moses's suggestion that he was afraid to cross-examine Scher about the shooting. "His story stank to high heaven," he boomed. "I couldn't improve on it. . . . You can't shoot somebody accidentally like that, there's no way in the world."

Campolongo brought up the ballistics tests, that all

the evidence showed that the shot was from at least three feet away. He reminded the jurors about the ammunition—the number 4 high brass—never used to skeet-shoot. He implored the jury to compare witnesses, to look at Justine Jenner's testimony versus Cindy Klein's. He pointed out that the former baby-sitter's story fit suspiciously well with Scher's testimony—that he was afraid of being wrongly accused because Marty's father was the mayor and he was the only Jew in town.

In the end, Robert Campolongo outlined what he believed the evidence had proved—that Marty, sunglasses and ear protectors on, had been caught completely unawares when Scher pulled the trigger. He maintained that Scher's story about an argument over the affair was bogus and that Scher lied when he said he tried to save Marty, to perform cardiac massage. To prove his point, the prosecutor held up an enlarged photograph of the body of Martin Dillon at Gunsmoke. Beside the victim, next to his hand, was a clay pigeon, unbroken. Nearby were the blood-spattered sunglasses and ear protectors.

"There couldn't have been any discussion," he charged. "He had ear protectors on! They weren't talking. It's nonsense. It doesn't fit. It doesn't make sense. You don't need an expert to tell you that. What was he doing? What was the poor man doing? Did we forget about the clay pigeons?"

At this point, Pat Scher began to cry softly.

"Those are the tell-tale clues," Campolongo practically shouted. "It was an execution! You don't have an accidental bullseye right in the center of the heart. Give me a break—it's fantasy land. . . . Look at the pictures. They're telling you something. The ear protectors, covered with blood. Look at the shirt. It's buttoned. He didn't have to stick his hand in there. He didn't have to check. It was one of his Hollywood acts. Look at the handkerchief. Did you hear him say he wiped off the barrel? If it's an accident, you fall on the gun, he should have left the blood.

"False in one thing, false in all things," he concluded. "A liar is a liar is a liar is a liar. A leopard doesn't change its spots. He was infatuated. He was obsessed with taking Marty Dillon's whole family, stripping him of his life. . . . This defendant, 'I'm going to get what I want. I believe in the religion of Stephen Scher, the religion of self. I get away with the affair.' His arrogance almost worked. He got away for 20 years. . . . The supreme gall, the arrogance. We have a man who thinks he can do whatever he wants and get away with it."

The senior deputy attorney general's voice quieted as he ended his closing argument by reminding the jury about Martin Dillon. He wanted them to think about him, to understand the young lawyer.

"I don't think Marty believed he was capable of this," he told the jury. "He's thinking, 'It's over, my wife chose me.' He was not confrontational, not a violent man. He was hoping it would burn itself out. When this thing was resolved in his favor, he had a smile on his face. He could go shooting because this guy had lost."

"Stephen Scher," Robert Campolongo said as he pointed to the defendant. "The evidence has stripped you naked, and you are guilty of first-degree murder."

He turned to the jury. "We ask you to find him so."

*　　*　　*

That night, Robert Campolongo and his team gathered at the Montrose House bar. Their job was done. A crowd gathered, and well-wishers thanked the prosecutor and his assistants for working so hard on the case.

Kendall Strawn showed up with his girlfriend, Debbie Taylor, and Morris Baker, one of Marty's old friends, arrived as well, buying drinks all around. Later that evening, the senior deputy attorney general took his group—Lt. Frank Hacken, deputy attorney general Bob O'Hara, deputy attorney general Marianne Kreisher, special agent Ted Bugda, trooper Jamie Schultz, and Irene Cushman, the team's paralegal—to the Choconut Inn for clams. The inn's owners toasted the prosecution team and gave them all baseball caps. When they returned to the hotel, Montrose House owner Rick Rose told his bartender, Pat Sheffler, that the drinks were on the house.

The next morning, Judge Kenneth Seamans charged the jury, and by ten-thirty the twelve men and women started deliberations. Larry and Jo Dillon went home to wait. Around noon, Jo Dillon announced that she was taking a walk to Holy Name of Mary Catholic Church a few blocks away. "I hope you need to come pick me up," she told her husband and friends.

They didn't. By the time she returned, there still had been no word from the courthouse.

Then, at three o'clock, the Dillons learned that a note had been passed to the judge: The jury had a question.

As word spread, reporters and locals who had gathered at the Public Avenue Deli hurried to the courthouse. The jury's request was simple, yet revealing.

They wanted an explanation of the different counts: first- and third-degree murder, involuntary manslaughter, and homicide by misadventure.

It was not a good sign for the defense. Clearly, the jury was not headed toward an acquittal.

Stephen Scher, his wife, and stepchildren returned to the home of Pat's relatives. But half an hour later they learned that the jury had sent the judge a final note. Throughout the area, local television news interrupted programming to announce that a verdict had been reached.

As word spread, the Public Avenue Deli quickly emptied as reporters and locals who'd gathered there to wait hurried to the courthouse. Deli owner Beverly Kinsey hung up her apron and flipped a Closed sign on the door and followed the crowd.

It was 5:05 p.m. Everyone in the courtroom stood as the seven women and five men on the jury slowly filed in. Stephen Scher sat forward in his chair at the defense table, his face tense, his mouth half-open. In the second row, Pat Scher, flanked by her children, held rosary beads and stared straight ahead. Larry and Jo Dillon, Joann and Alan Reimel, the Nashes and Lynches, all sat in their usual places, holding hands. At the prosecution table, deputy attorney general Bob O'Hara glanced at the jurors and scrawled two words on a piece of paper and folded it over.

Then, in the silent courtroom Jury Foreman Judd Holbrook rose. In a clear voice he announced the finding of the jury on the most serious count, murder in the first degree.

"Guilty."

A gasp was heard and from outside on the street a cheer echoed. Standing in the corner of the courtroom, Peter Loftus, the Dillon's attorney, silently thrust his arms in the air in a sign of victory, and upstairs, in the balcony, Ann Vitale dropped her head and tears began streaming down her face. At the prosecution's table, Bob O'Hara turned to the prosecution team's appeals expert, Marianne Kreisher, and unfolded the paper, revealing what he'd scrawled moments before the verdict was read. *First Degree.*

Neither Steve and Pat Scher nor Larry and Jo Dillon showed any reaction. Michael and Suzanne, too, sat expressionless.

Then, Robert Campolongo, his voice unsteady for the first time during the trial, stood to address the court.

"We have justice, thanks be to God," the prosecutor declared. "God bless this jury for doing justice, God bless them every one. This is the time of reckoning after 20 years."

He asked Judge Seamans to immediately impose a life sentence on the defendant. But an agitated John Moses objected, informing Judge Seamans that he planned to file an appeal right away and that he opposed a sentencing occur that day. The defense attorney stressed that despite the jury's verdict, the family of Stephen Scher stood solidly behind him.

The judge called the attorneys to a sidebar. As they approached the bench, Bob O'Hara had a moment alone with Robert Campolongo.

"Before everyone starts blowing smoke up your ass, I want you to know I was very proud to work with you," he told his boss. "You did an excellent job. Your closing was one of the best I've seen."

As the attorneys and the judge discussed the sentencing, Joann Reimel could no longer control her emotions. She got out of her seat and walked over to her father, in his usual place at the end of the aisle. She leaned over, and buried her head in his shoulder. Not a sound was heard from her, yet it was clear she was sobbing.

On the other side of the courtroom, Pat, Michael, and Suzanne stared at her. No one said a word.

CHAPTER 24

When Judge Seamans asked John Moses if his client wished to address the court, the attorney indicated his client did.

Standing next to his lawyer, Stephen Scher spoke so softly he could barely be heard. "Your Honor, I understand the workings of the court and the finding of the jury," he said, his hands clasped in front of him. "I would like to say the testimony I gave was truthful."

With that, Stephen Scher turned around and faced the second row on the left side of the courtroom where Michael and Suzanne sat motionless next to their mother. "I did not kill the father of my children," Stephen Scher said, looking directly at them. "I maintain my innocence."

There was no reaction from the Dillon children or from Pat Scher.

Moments later, Judge Seamans imposed the sentence. "Stephen Barry Scher, the jury having found you guilty, I hereby sentence you to eternal life in prison at the state correctional facility."

Sheriff Dick Pelicci handcuffed the doctor and along with several state troopers led him out of the courtroom. Judge Seamans rose from the bench. The proceedings were over.

Instantly, reporters and well-wishers crowded around Larry and Jo Dillon and Joann and Alan Reimel. When asked by reporters for his emotions at the moment, Larry Dillon clutched his cane and practically whispered his response. "I feel okay. Once in a while it was a little rough."

Jo Dillon told the press that the ordeal brought them closure, but no happiness. "I prayed this day would come. I'm so relieved it's over, but I have no joy, because we've lost our grandchildren."

Larry Dillon nodded. "We still love them," he said quietly. "We'll wait to hear from them."

Shelly Wolfe, Jo Dillon's niece, added, "We look forward to the day that Michael and Suzanne at least understand why their grandfather did this before he died."

Minutes later, a crowd gathered by the back entrance to the courthouse as Sheriff Dick Pelicci led Scher to a waiting car, bound for the Susquehanna County jail. When the doctor emerged, several onlookers cheered and applauded. Upstairs in the courthouse, Pat Scher watched from a window. "You bastards," she said through gritted teeth.

Reverend Farwell stood by Pat's side, equally bitter. "Just listen to the cheers," he snapped angrily to a reporter. "Honest to God. A man has been separated from his family."

*   *   *

After Scher's departure, Joann Reimel and Shelly Wolfe headed across a small park to the Montrose firehouse, followed by a small army of supporters and television crews. The crowd grew silent as a weeping Joann Reimel declared, "This is for my brother."

Her cousin Shelly began to push the old fire bell, rusted from years of disuse. In the cool evening air, the bell tolled twenty-one times, signaling each year since the death of Marty Dillon.

An echo remained at the end, seemingly hanging in the air. By now, Bonnie Mead and Tom Sivahop had pulled up to the firehouse. The couple had been en route to Montrose from Tom's home in Wilkes-Barre when they heard the verdict on the car radio.

In front of the firehouse, Bonnie and Joann embraced. Then Paul Kelly, the local attorney who'd grown up with Marty, arrived and presented the secretary a trophy he and his wife, Pam, had made in anticipation of a guilty verdict. It read: "Bonnie Mead: Wow, you were right!"

"It's justice," Bonnie said, waving the trophy and hugging her friends, one by one. "It's about time."

Joann nodded, wiping away tears. "My big thing is my brother," she told the gathering, pointing to the sky. "He did this from up there. But he had to do it through Mr. Campolongo. On June 2, 1976, it was between a doctor and a lawyer, and the doctor won that day. But today, the lawyer won."

Later, Robert Campolongo, Bob O'Hara, Lieutenant Hacken, and the troopers stopped by Joann and Alan Reimel's home where a small crowd of the Dillons' friends and family had gathered. That evening, at the Montrose House, Bob O'Hara and the others mused about Stephen Scher's curious words during the sentencing. O'Hara noted the odd way the doctor referred to Marty Dillon, as "the father of my children."

"That's what profilers tell you—to look for the way suspects give their statements," O'Hara said to the others, who nodded in agreement. "They don't use proper names and they put some distance between themselves and the victim. It tells you something."

The following evening, Larry and Jo hosted a buffet for about forty people at the Montrose House to thank everyone for all they'd done. Kerry Graham and Kendall Strawn came, and so did Bonnie Mead, Tom Sivahop, Robert Bartron, and members of the state police and the attorney general's office.

The Dillons made it clear they did not consider the dinner a celebration. "There is no joy," Jo's cousin Bill Nash explained to a reporter. "A man going to jail for life is a sad, sad thing. The family members weren't present for the cheering. We would never have done that."

At the dinner, Bob O'Hara shook Larry Dillon's hand, and embraced Jo Dillon. He told the couple he was very glad to have met them and thanked them for their support during the trial. Jo Dillon reminded him of his own mother, always encouraging and optimistic. Throughout the trial she repeatedly told the prosecutors and state police how much she appreciated their work, and that regardless of how the verdict turned out, she thought they had done an excellent job.

Midway through the dinner, O'Hara went to get some punch and noticed a collage of photographs of Marty that Larry and Jo had assembled in the back of the dining room. Among them was a 1968 wedding picture of a smiling Marty Dillon and his new bride, Patty Karveller. But it was an enlarged black and white photo of Marty with three year old Michael on his lap, the two faces intently looking at each other, away from the camera, that moved O'Hara most.

The prosecutor couldn't take his eyes off the image of the young lawyer, just about his age, and his boy. O'Hara, too, had a young son, Ryan. He felt a well of emotion swell within him. Then, Ann Vitale walked over and stood beside him. Her eyes, too, quickly filled with tears.

"That's what this was all about," O'Hara said quietly, and Stephen Scher's former wife nodded.

The next morning, the prosecution team packed up their belongings and at last checked out of Montrose House, saying good-bye to owners Rick and Candy Rose. Michael Giangrieco, the coroner's solicitor, helped Troopers Steve Stoud and Jamie Schultz load boxes of files from the prosecutor's third-floor office into their cars for the trip back to Harrisburg. The three men discussed the verdict.

"He sealed his fate when he took the stand and lied again," Giangrieco said with a shrug. "What he said didn't fit the evidence. That's why it didn't take long to convict him. There're no winners in this. It's a tragic situation for both families."

At the Public Avenue Deli, where hordes had gathered every day, it was quiet for the first time in months. Throughout the day, owners Beverly and Henry Kinsey chatted with customers about the outcome of the trial. Beverly had been one of the first to hug Jo Dillon after the verdict was read. She felt a particular kinship with the older woman—Beverly, too, had lost a child, more than a decade earlier. Her eight-year-old daughter had suddenly developed a virus and by the time she was rushed to the hospital it was too late. It had been important to Beverly to know all the details of why her child died. She understood how much that, too, must have meant to the Dillons.

"They finally got their answer, which is what Larry and Jo deserved," Beverly told customers.

Within days of her husband's conviction, Pat Scher drove ten hours home to Lincolnton to pick up Jonathan and almost immediately turned around and brought him back to Montrose. She stayed on for several more days at her relatives' home, meeting with John Moses in Wilkes-Barre to discuss the appeal.

She bid an emotional good-bye to her children as they flew to their respective homes, Michael to Las Cruces, Suzanne to Colorado Springs. For the second time in their lives, the Dillon children had lost a father.

Michael seemed to bear his pain quietly, but Suzanne did not. A month after her stepfather's conviction, the young woman wrote a scathing letter to the editor of the *Susquehanna Transcript,* lashing out at the newspaper and the Montrose community for creating a circus atmosphere and for decimating her family.

> *My brother and I struggle to keep our head above the surface of the water, and fight desperately to keep our mother and younger brother up there with us. Our lives have been destroyed, not just Stephen Scher's. My mother. My little brother. The Dillon family. Think about that as you ring the firehouse bell and cheer. Think about how peaceful my father's rest must be watching his children suffer so. Think about it as you smugly relive the drama and excite-*

ment of your participation in the spectacle.
Congratulations. Good job. You won.
Suzanne R. Dillon

There was even more pain to befall the Dillon children. Just two months after the stepfather's conviction, their mother was charged with a crime as well—two felony counts of perjury, two counts of making false statements under oath, and obstruction of the administration of the law—for lying about her affair with Stephen Scher. It was in a 1995 deposition to the Dillon's attorney, Peter Loftus, in which she made that claim, hoping to halt the exhumation proceedings by dispelling the possibility of a motive for Stephen Scher to have killed Marty Dillon. For several weeks after Scher's conviction, Susquehanna District Attorney Charles Aliano, weighed whether to bring charges against Pat. In the end, he did.

"We can't have people lying in court," he told reporter Carol Crane from the Wilkes Barre *Citizen's Voice* newspaper. "Our system is based upon people having respect for the oath they take."

After the trial ended, Larry and Jo Dillon concentrated on catching up with their daughter's three boys, attending the soccer and basketball games they'd neglected during the busy previous months. But the loss of their son's children remained a constant ache, a solemn reminder of the risk they took when they urged the state police to investigate Marty's death.

Yet God answered their prayers in the fall of 1997, when the police investigation revealed the truth about what happened at Gunsmoke and Dr. Stephen Scher was brought to justice. And now they wonder if there is a chance for another miracle—that one day their grandchildren will return to them. Larry and Jo will wait for Michael and Suzanne. Their patience was rewarded once before.

Today, the ironwood tree at Gunsmoke still bears a small ovoid scar from where Stephen Scher smashed the Winchester, and a plain iron cross embedded in a granite boulder marks the spot where Marty Dillon died. The trailer is gone now, a spacious cabin in its place, with black-and-white photos of Marty hanging on the walls. Most days, Larry and Jo feed the deer in the woods apples that Bill Nash brings them from his orchard, and they sit on the front porch and read. They still walk up to to the clearing at Gunsmoke and visit Holy Name of Mary Cemetery, both the unmarked grave where their son is buried, and the site of his tombstone. On it, beneath the name *Martin Thomas Dillon*, is etched a phrase from the Book of Wisdom, the irony of which is not lost on Larry and Jo Dillon and all those who loved a young lawyer named Marty in the hilltop town of Montrose, Pennsylvania, back in 1976.

The just man, though he die early, shall be at rest.